TRACING YOUR ANCESTORS THROUGH LOCAL HISTORY RECORDS

FAMILY HISTORY FROM PEN & SWORD

Tracing Your Army Ancestors
Simon Fowler
•

Tracing Your Pauper Ancestors
Robert Burlison
•

Tracing Your Yorkshire Ancestors
Rachel Bellerby
•

Tracing Your Air Force Ancestors
Phil Tomaselli
•

Tracing Your Northern Ancestors
Keith Gregson
•

*Tracing Your Black Country
Ancestors*
Michael Pearson
•

Tracing Your Textile Ancestors
Vivien Teasdale
•

Tracing Your Railway Ancestors
Di Drummond
•

Tracing Secret Service Ancestors
Phil Tomaselli
•

Tracing Your Police Ancestors
Stephen Wade
•

*Tracing Your Royal Marine
Ancestors*
Richard Brooks
and Matthew Little
•

Tracing Your Jewish Ancestors
Rosemary Wenzerul
•

*Tracing Your East Anglian
Ancestors*
Gill Blanchard
•

Tracing Your Ancestors
Simon Fowler
•

Tracing Your Liverpool Ancestors
Mike Royden
•

Tracing Your Scottish Ancestors
Ian Maxwell
•

*Tracing British Battalions on the
Somme*
Ray Westlake
•

Tracing Your Criminal Ancestors
Stephen Wade
•

*Tracing Your Labour Movement
Ancestors*
Mark Crail
•

Tracing Your London Ancestors
Jonathan Oates
•

*Tracing Your Shipbuilding
Ancestors*
Anthony Burton
•

*Tracing Your Northern Irish
Ancestors*
Ian Maxwell
•

*Tracing Your Service Women
Ancestors*
Mary Ingham
•

Tracing Your East End Ancestors
Jane Cox
•

Tracing the Rifle Volunteers
Ray Westlake
•

Tracing Your Legal Ancestors
Stephen Wade
•

Tracing Your Canal Ancestors
Sue Wilkes
•

Tracing Your Rural Ancestors
Jonathan Brown
•

Tracing Your House History
Gill Blanchard
•

Tracing Your Tank Ancestors
Janice Tait and David Fletcher
•

*Tracing Your Family History on
the Internet*
Chris Paton
•

*Tracing Your Medical
Ancestors*
Michelle Higgs
•

*Tracing Your Second World War
Ancestors*
Phil Tomaselli
•

*Tracing Your Channel Islands
Ancestors*
Marie-Louise Backhurst
•

*Tracing Great War Ancestors
DVD*
Pen & Sword Digital &
Battlefield History TV Ltd
•

*Tracing Your Prisoner of War
Ancestors: The First World War*
Sarah Paterson
•

*Tracing Your British Indian
Ancestors*
Emma Jolly
•

*Tracing Your Naval
Ancestors*
Simon Fowler
•

Tracing Your Huguenot Ancestors
Kathy Chater
•

Tracing Your Servant Ancestors
Michelle Higgs
•

*Tracing Your Ancestors from 1066
to 1837*
Jonathan Oates
•

*Tracing Your Merchant Navy
Ancestors*
Simon Wills
•

*Tracing Your Lancashire
Ancestors*
Sue Wilkes
•

*Tracing Your Ancestors through
Death Records*
Celia Heritage
•

*Tracing Your West Country
Ancestors*
Kirsty Gray
•

*Tracing Your First World War
Ancestors*
Simon Fowler
•

*Tracing Your Army Ancestors –
2nd Edition*
Simon Fowler
•

*Tracing Your Irish Family History
on the Internet*
Chris Paton
•

*Tracing Your Aristocratic
Ancestors*
Anthony Adolph
•

*Tracing Your Ancestors from 1066
to 1837*
Jonathan Oates
•

TRACING YOUR ANCESTORS THROUGH LOCAL HISTORY RECORDS

A Guide for Family Historians

Jonathan Oates

Pen & Sword
FAMILY HISTORY

First published in Great Britain in 2016
PEN & SWORD FAMILY HISTORY
an imprint of
Pen & Sword Books Ltd
47 Church Street,
Barnsley
South Yorkshire,
S70 2AS

ISBN 978 1 47383 802 4

Typeset in Palatino and Optima by CHIC GRAPHICS

Printed and bound in England by
CPI Group (UK), Croydon, CR0 4YY

Pen & Sword Books Ltd incorporates the imprints of Pen & Sword
Archaeology, Atlas, Aviation, Battleground, Discovery, Family History,
History, Maritime, Military, Naval, Politics, Railways, Select, Social History,
Transport, True Crime, Claymore Press, Frontline Books, Leo Cooper,
Praetorian Press, Remember When, Seaforth Publishing and Wharncliffe.

For a complete list of Pen & Sword titles please contact
PEN & SWORD BOOKS LTD
47 Church Street, Barnsley, South Yorkshire, S70 2AS, England
E-mail: enquiries@pen-and-sword.co.uk
Website: www.pen-and-sword.co.uk

CONTENTS

ACKNOWLEDGEMENTS

I would like to thank fellow archivist Ruth Costello for having read through the draft and having made many helpful suggestions. Paul Lang, who has read the text, has also, as always, been kind in assisting with pictures from his vast collection. Vanda Foster read over Chapter 11 and provided guidance and assistance there. Any errors, are, of course, my own responsibility.

This book is dedicated to Ruth.

LIST OF ILLUSTRATIONS

Whitchurch Silk Mill, Hampshire, 2014 (Author)
Monumental inscription at St Peter's church, Iver, 2015 (Author)
St Peter's church, Iver, 2015 (Author)
Highgate Cemetery certificate, 1855 (Paul Lang)
Advert for local football match (Paul Lang)
Trade token (Paul Lang)
Shop front in Horsham Museum, 2014 (Author)
Dr Johnson's House Museum (Paul Lang)
Interior of Oxford Prison Museum (Author)
Horsham Museum, 2014 (Author)
Thomas Faulkner, local historian (London Borough of Ealing)

INTRODUCTION

This is not a book for the beginner in family history, someone whose enthusiasm has been kindled, perhaps by *Who Do You Think You Are?* Rather, it is envisaged that the reader will be someone who has already constructed a family tree, perhaps going back centuries, and has names, places and dates at their command, a task that often takes years. For many, though, these ancestors are just names, potentially mere two-dimensional figures at best. This book, therefore, is for those who want to know more about their ancestors' lives and times in order to flesh them out more fully. It does so by exploring the topic of local history. Local and family history are often seen as two different disciplines. But it was not always so and need not be the case now.

The roots of the study of both local history and family history stretch back several centuries. By local history what is meant is the study of a locality's past; whether it be of a county, city, town or parish (or even a whole region, for example, the northwest of England), as opposed to national or international history, which is the mainstay of the educational curriculum or history in the media. Within that remit, such a history may be very specific, such as a history of a particular topic, for instance, the impact of a world war on a community, a local industry or political movement, or may be more ambitious, an attempt to cover centuries of a town's history. It may be the work of amateur historians or those who are professionals. Unlike family history, research often results in publication, either by a publishing house or self-published. It may be mainly made up of illustrations or may be primarily text-based. Local histories exist in prodigious numbers and there can be few places in Britain which have not been covered by a local history book and a Wikipedia website, of varying quality and age.

The materials for these histories, are, as with those for family history, numerous and varied and not to be found in one place. Many are, of course, located in the county or borough record office or in the reference section of county and city libraries. Others are held at the National Archives or specialist repositories. Finally, there is also value in viewing the place itself, though remembering that much will have altered throughout the ages, depending on the locality.

By now the reader may well be asking what local history has to do with family history. After all, the local and the family historian are looking for different subject matter; the former for the history of a place and its inhabitants, the latter for a particular individual or family. At one time, record office staff would categorise the two types of researcher as being wholly different (perhaps some still do).

Yet it is increasingly recognised that there is no hard and fast distinction between the two topics. Both concern the activities and experiences of people in the past. Family history should be about more than names and the often relatively scanty information which is usually all that can be discovered about specific individuals unless they were extremely notorious, rich or well-known by contemporaries for other reasons. The topics intersect.

This is no new observation, for the editorial of the first issue of *The Amateur Historian* (later renamed *The Local Historian*) noted, in 1952, the connection between the two:

> The amateur [historian] … directs his attention to smaller and more personal fields, his family, his locality, his institutions. These fields overlap; the genealogist needs to study the place in which his ancestors lived; the local historian draws much of his information from archaeology and family records.

An important dimension is lost if that individual or family is isolated from their surroundings. As the metaphysical poet, John Donne, wrote,

No man is an island
Entire of itself.
Every man is a piece of the continent,
A part of the Main.

We are all influenced by the immediate society in which we live, work, play and worship; by the way we travel and who our neighbours are. Our ancestors were no different. In many ways they were more so. Until the 1950s there was, for most people, little in the way of home entertainment. People's housing conditions, too, were often far from tolerable. Most would spend their leisure hours with their fellows. For better or worse, social intercourse on a face to face basis was far more important then than it is in our increasingly digital age.

In order to find out about this extra dimension of our ancestors' lives, we need to examine the materials for the study of the neighbourhoods in which our ancestors lived. We will probably not find anything directly about them – though this is a possibility – but will learn more about the framework of their lives and thus about them and the society they lived in. This book will help you to do so.

We will begin with a chapter about England's history, paying close attention to administrative, ecclesiastical and social developments, which provide a framework to our ancestors' lives. We also need to know a little about the origins and development of local history from the sixteenth century onwards. Then we will look at the specific sources for local history, their location and their value for family historians. There will be chapters covering maps, photographs, illustrations, newspapers, books, ephemera and archives. There will be a chapter about sources for local historian at the National Archives and other national and regional repositories. Another chapter will discuss the value of fieldwork. Museums and their contents will be examined.

The author has worked as an archivist in local government for two decades and has assisted many local and family historians. He has written several books about local and regional history (for both the popular and academic markets) as well as on family history. He is therefore ideally placed to share his knowledge of local history sources.

This book is primarily a guide to sources in England. This is because those institutions in church and state which have and do produce archives elsewhere in Britain are different to those in England (Scotland retained its own church and judiciary post-Union, for example), so would need additional space to do justice to them. Furthermore, they are largely outside this author's experience and knowledge. However, the book does refer to institutions which cover the whole kingdom, such as the National Archives and Parliamentary Archives, as well as the material on other topics such as maps and photographs.

Let us take an example as to how this book will be of use, by taking an imaginary family in an imagined county. The family historian knows that at the time of the census in 1881 his ancestor, the Revd John Derby, is residing with his family at the Vicarage, Church Lane, in the village of Mudchester in Middleshire. He is 35 years old and his wife Anne is 31. They have four children aged between 1 and 9 years old, and two domestic servants; the children and the servants being born in Mudchester, Derby in Hanwell, Oxfordshire, and his wife in Reading, Berkshire. Ten years later, the 1891 census notes the two Derby adults as still present at that address, but with two different servants, whilst only two of the children are still listed there (all aged another 10 years). Parish registers and civil registration certificates give the dates of births and marriages.

This is all to the good, but it is basic. It is a skeleton, but meat can be put on the bones to help bring colour to the lives of these people. What were the family doing between the census years (apart from mourning the child who died in 1884)? What was their life like? What might they have witnessed? There can be no hard and fast answers, but an investigation into the sources for the history of the village in which they lived may provide clues.

Perhaps we might begin by looking at the physical environment in which the family lived. Photographs and postcards exist which depict the village in the late nineteenth and early twentieth centuries. There are some which show the parish church before it was burnt down in 1920 and rebuilt with a spire, for instance. Some of the postcards show horse-drawn traffic which the Derbys would have known about and seen. There is also a photograph showing a crowd scene in which flags and crowns are prominent, but no other clue as to when this might have been. Another source might be needed to explore the story behind the card.

Could this have been a village celebration of Queen Victoria's Jubilee of 1887? It is worth checking the county newspaper, *The Middleshire Gazette*. This newspaper carried a special supplement for the Jubilee week and, though there are no photographs, there is a column detailing the festivities organised in several of the villages. Fortunately there is a column for Mudchester. It refers to a large pig being roasted, organised games for the children, a special tea for the old folk and buildings festooned with flags and other appropriate memorabilia. There is even a reference to a sermon by the Revd Derby on the occasion. Of course, in searching through the editions of the newspaper, it is impossible not to read about other events in the county and even in the village itself (which as with other villages often has a few paragraphs about very localised news). Poaching seems to have been a frequent issue, judging by the reports of the hearings of the Assize courts. There are also adverts for servants, stating experience needed, sex and wages. Perhaps the Derbys paid their servants these wages and conditions.

But there are too few pictures of the village at or around the time that our family dwelt there, so they alone do not give a very comprehensive feel for the place and the family's location within it. What we need are maps. The 1894 Ordnance Survey map is the nearest in time (the early edition of the 1860s one is a little early). Placing two OS sheets together gives us most of the village and outlying hamlets. We can see that the vicarage is rather to the south of the railway line. The latter is surrounded by most of the housing including the High Street and local Board Offices, as well as a Methodist chapel and a school. Much of the map shows outlying farms, surrounded by fields and trackways. The early edition of the map does not show the railway line and depicts the majority of the houses as being to the south, close to the church and vicarage. We may deduce, perhaps, that the railway line helped stimulate demand for housing in its immediate environs, and rapid population expansion, and that the time of the Derbys' residence coincided with some of this great upheaval to this hitherto rural community.

When did all this occur? All the maps will tell us is that it was between 1865 and 1894. Another source is needed. One method is to check the editions of the Kelly's directories for the period. As these were produced annually and list streets and householders, they record the building of new streets and their expansion over time. The directories also provide a concise summary for each village and these give the figures for each census and thus indicate that the period between 1881 and 1891 saw a doubling of its population.

There is other information to be found about local life. The County Record Office has the archives of the Mudchester Local Board as well as the Vestry Minute Books of the parish of which Derby was vicar. The Local Board was founded in 1885 to deal with health, sewerage, lighting and the local roads, as its minutes record. It seems that they had the first gas lighting installed, first along the High Street and then, much later, along some of the newly built thoroughfares. Clearly, the village must have been in almost complete darkness after the sun set until 1885. Drainage began to be dug for sewerage in the 1890s. The Vestry meetings, which were chaired by Derby, detail various aspects of repair work done to the church and improvements to the churchyard wall.

Among the records held at the National Archives at Kew there is a Home Office file about an outbreak of cattle blinding that had taken place in adjacent parishes in 1889. There are notices sent by the Home Office to a number of parishes in Middleshire among which was Mudchester, with recommendations for precautions to be observed and for collaboration with the county constabulary.

We know that Mudchester is a farming community. One of the best places to learn about life in the English countryside is the Centre for Rural Life at Reading University. This has machinery and implements from farms long ago. There is also literature, ephemera and oral history recordings of people who worked on the land in the past. There may also be a county or town museum, for Mudchester is now a large town compared to its village status in the late nineteenth century and amongst the exhibits there may well be three-dimensional objects for the years that the Derbys lived there. These may be from shops or workshops; quite possibly part of one of these places may have been recreated in the museum.

It is also worth visiting Mudchester itself. Before a visit it is worth doing some background reading. Few places lack a local history book or at least a book showing the town or village in old photographs. The appropriate volume of the *Middleshire Victoria County History* (available online at British History online) or in the county archives or library as a paper copy should also supply relevant information. Finally the Pevsner volume on the extant buildings of the place will provide guidance on what exists now. These books indicate that the Georgian Vicarage was sold by the diocese in the 1970s, but still exists and is known as The Old Vicarage. Contacting the present owners and explaining your interest in the property might result in an offer of a visit there.

In any case, armed with all this information, and perhaps a copy of a map, an itinerary can then be planned. A visit to the church itself is a crucial part of the visit, and so it should be ascertained in advance whether the church is usually open outside service times or whether the clergyman or churchwardens can provide access out of hours as it were. Armed with a camera as well as books and maps, an examination of those properties in existence at the time of your ancestors' residence can be most rewarding. Some of the older properties will still survive and some may be still used for their original purpose. Others may be in existence, but have a new purpose; the old school may well have become too small for the rising school population and now be a community centre, or additional buildings may have been added to the original one. Shops may sell different goods and have radically different frontages, but look up and you will see some of the original buildings that the Derbys knew.

There are other sources of information, too. Local studies libraries or local museums may have other pieces of the jigsaw puzzle. There may be scraps of evidence known as ephemera – such as receipts or invoices for transactions in local shops or even advertising posters and handbills. At election time candidates had literature distributed and these may have survived. All these give more insight into life in the Derbys' time. It is also worth checking whether there are any oral history recordings of people who remembered life in the village in the late nineteenth century. These may well be by 'ordinary' people whose voices and opinions may be recorded nowhere else.

Books published at the time also give an impression of how a particular place was during a particular year. County and local directories list shops and institutions in a place; many villages had shops selling agricultural produce and smithies were not uncommon. Parish magazines – of clear importance for a clergy family – list groups supported by the church. These often include women's and children's groups, social and sporting clubs as well as Bible classes and missionary work. Finally, Medical Officer of Health reports give insights into health issues affecting a district, giving statistics of causes of death and infant mortality, comments on the effects of increased building (and as Mudchester was expanding rapidly in the 1880s these are particularly pertinent).

Thus by using sources for the local history of Mudchester, quite a lot has been learnt about the physical environment of the Derbys, about the little world which they were part of and which they knew very well indeed.

Chapter 1

A BRIEF HISTORY OF ENGLAND

Local history is not the history generally taught in schools and universities, nor in books or on television. What we normally see is national history, the dramas of kings and queens, of politicians and soldiers, and other 'Great Men and Women'. Yet most people lived in small agricultural communities where communication and travel were far more limited than in recent decades. Emigration and immigration occurred on a far smaller scale. The following chapter will attempt a brief overview of local history from the Middle Ages to the twentieth century. A good website for an overall history of Britain is www. bbc.co.uk/history/british.

Medieval England, 1066–1485

England, as a political entity with defined borders, came about in the Anglo-Saxon period, and in the tenth century, with the defeat of the Viking incursions, at least temporarily, the establishment of borders with Wales and Scotland, and the unification of the Saxon kingdoms into one, under the House of Wessex. Counties were beginning to be formed in the seventh and eighth centuries, chiefly in the south of England. After 1066, others were formed and these 39 counties became the administrative building blocks of the English state up until the 1970s. They varied considerably in size and population, with Yorkshire, Lincolnshire and Devon being the largest and Rutland and Middlesex being the smallest. However the latter contained the most populous city in the country, London. In the Middle Ages, the county's chief secular officer in the King's interest was the sheriff, responsible for law and order, and for many is best, if unfairly, represented by the Sheriff of Nottingham in the Robin Hood stories.

Religion was a major influence on the life of our ancestors. Arguably it was the most important and it is essential that readers should remember this. Christianity was re-established in England in the seventh and eight centuries and the old pagan gods were eventually vanquished. Everyone owed religious allegiance to the Pope, of course, until the Protestant reformation of the sixteenth century. It is difficult to exaggerate the power of the medieval church over all the kingdom's souls. There were two provinces; York and Canterbury and these were subdivided into dioceses (which rarely equated to the county system), then archdeaconries, then parishes (which, again, did not equate with manors). As well as the diocesan system, there were also the monastic houses of the Benedictine and Cistercian orders, to name but two of the more numerous. They maintained numerous abbeys, priories, monasteries, chantries and chapels throughout the country. In 1216 there were 700 religious houses and 13,000 monks and nuns; their numbers increased throughout the century. This was partly because of the increase in numbers of friaries. Abbots were leading tenants of the King and held many manors. Monasteries also maintained hospitals and libraries as well as being centres for the worship of God. The parish priest, by contrast, was a humble fellow; he farmed the land he held from the lord of the manor and was rarely celibate, until reforms later in the eleventh century.

Conway Castle. (Paul Lang)

CONWAY CASTLE AND BRIDGE,

Although the Norman Conquest resulted in a new monarch and a new aristocracy supplanting the old one (4,000 Saxon thegns were replaced by 200 barons), much remained the same. This was the feudal system in which the monarch was landholder in chief (under God) and his leading followers were his chief tenants, both nobility and churchmen, who held (not owned, at least in theory) land from him. This would usually be scattered throughout the kingdom rather than being one substantial swathe of territory. They had lesser tenants and so the process went downwards. In return for such land, the tenant owed his immediate superior service, often military, but increasingly as time went by, financial.

English society was overwhelmingly rural, with very few towns and cities. Most people lived and worked on the land in manors. The major groupings therein were the villeins, who held 45 per cent of land and made up 41 per cent of the population, then cottars, who held a mere 5 per cent of land but made up about 32 per cent of the population. Then there were the landless, about 9 per cent of the population. At the other end of the scale were freemen, making up 14 per cent of the population, but holding 20 per cent of land, and, of course, the tiny elite of barons and bishops. Most people worked in farming and fishing; the only industry of any importance was cloth. Very few people lived in towns; London had about 40,000 residents in the fifteenth century and most towns and cities counted residents in their thousands. Yet a number of boroughs were established by charters and they existed for administrative purposes outside the counties and were largely self-governed.

Government and society in the Middle Ages were far different to what they are today. National government was in the hands of the King and his council, with the former the most important figure in the political world. He could declare war, embark on diplomacy, choose his own servants and levy taxes. His wealth and powers of patronage were extensive and so could reward his supporters and promise rewards to others whose loyalty he required. He was not absolute, of course, and had to choose his friends and his policies carefully. Disastrous decisions and bad luck resulted in Edward II and Henry VI being deposed and murdered. The monarchy was not always hereditary at this time, though it often was. From 1154 to 1485 the monarchs were members of the House of Plantagenet.

Central government was minimal and it was also itinerant; the monarch moved about the country and his government moved with him. Yet, despite the growth in officials, there were still relatively few of what we would call civil servants. By the end of the fifteenth century government had become fixed at Westminster. Far more of the day-to-day administration was in the hands of urban corporations and manorial courts. Health and education were not the province of government, but of the church.

Law and order was a major preoccupation of the monarch and his government. In the twelfth century, Henry II instituted the Assizes system of courts which was to endure until 1971. These resulted in itinerant judges touring circuits, each made up of a number of adjacent counties, twice a year, to hear cases of serious crime. At local level, manorial courts upheld justice.

Parliament emerged in the thirteenth century, but was primarily a court of law rather than a fiscal institution. Taxation was not required on an annual basis, but for extraordinary expenditure, which usually meant paying for war. In peacetime, the monarch was expected to use his own resources, such as his crown lands, customs dues, feudal incidents and the profits of justice, and these provided the bulk of his revenue. Parliament had brief sittings and in the second half of the fifteenth century only met once every three years.

England's population fluctuated greatly. With between 1 and 2 million in 1066, it then grew steadily in the next centuries, perhaps reaching 5–7 million by 1300, but was cut savagely in the fourteenth century due to the Black Death. Possibly a third or half of the population died. By the end of the Middle Ages, numbers were about 2.5 million. The population was becoming increasingly literate and French, the language of government since the Conquest, was replaced by English in the fourteenth century.

By the end of the Middle Ages the English state had incorporated Wales as a principality and claimed sovereignty over Ireland and Scotland, though most of the overseas possessions of the Norman and Plantagenet monarchies of the eleventh and twelfth centuries had been lost. It was an increasingly self-confident, though small, nation.

Tudor and Stuart England, 1485–1714

Henry VII, the first of the Tudor monarchs, following his decisive victory at Bosworth and the death in battle of his predecessor, Richard III, continued the attempts of Edward IV to strengthen the monarchy, both financially and judicially, though there was still no standing army or police force. Henry introduced legal and judicial methods such as the Court of Star Chamber, to rule England and to make the crown stronger and richer than the chief landowners. Tudor government saw a shift from the medieval towards the more bureaucratic form of government which we are more accustomed to now, but we should not exaggerate this revolution as much stayed the same.

The key change was the relation between church and state which culminated in the dissolution of the monastic houses in the 1530s and

Ruins of Tintern Abbey. (Paul Lang)

made the monarch head of the church, rather than the Pope. This led to church and state being linked, with the same individual at the head of both. At the bottom level of both was the parish, and its responsibilities rose throughout the century. There was also a major redistribution of landed power as monastic land was bought or given to the nobility and the gentry, the latter becoming increasingly an important force in politics.

Henry VIII was the head of a Catholic Church; however he was his own 'Pope'. It was during his son's brief reign that the Protestant reformation made state-sponsored progress. Although this was interrupted by his Catholic sister Mary's equally brief reign, a compromise of sorts was reached under Elizabeth. The Church of England became Protestant, though not of a radical brand as desired by some. Equally, the Catholic faith was under attack. This was increasingly the case as the century drew on and England became involved with wars with foreign Catholic powers, chiefly Spain. There were some alterations to the diocesan structure, such as the creation of the diocese of Chester, but the system changed but little.

Religious radicalism had helped lead to the reformation, but was also a result of it, too. There were many Protestants who refused to acknowledge the sovereignty of the monarchy. Initially these were termed Puritans. Their fortunes waxed and waned over this period and perhaps reached their zenith in the 1650s when the Anglican Church, deprived of monarch and bishops, was at its weakest. Yet the Restoration of 1660 resulted in nonconformists being penalised, as they had been since 1559. They could not worship legally and faced fines and imprisonment. The Bill of Rights of 1689 led to a limited toleration of nonconformist worship, though full political, educational and civil equality was not achieved until the early nineteenth century. Not everyone turned towards Protestantism in any form. There were some who clung to Catholicism, especially in parts of northern England. As with nonconformists, their political and civic rights were limited, as were their religious ones.

Parliament grew in strength as a political entity in these centuries, though this was not preordained as monarchs had ruled without it in 1629–40, 1681–5 and 1685–8, and it was, ironically, much reduced in power during the Commonwealth years. Parliament's importance was not merely legislative but fiscal. The monarch could no longer live without direct taxation as the cost of government rose, especially if he or she wanted to maintain a standing army and conduct an interventionist foreign policy. By 1689 it was an indispensable political institution.

This is not to say that the monarchy's powers were vastly reduced. They were still expected to rule as well as reign. They could declare war or conduct diplomacy. They could choose their own ministers. They had an immense amount of patronage at their disposal. However they had to work in partnership with Parliament; not always an easy task, but by the time of William III (1689–1702), they could do so without the major quarrels which, under the earlier Stuarts, had led to civil war in 1642.

Local administration increasingly passed into the hands of the justices of the peace at quarter sessions and the parish and away from the sheriff and the manor, though these institutions remained. Social and economic legislation was entrusted to these bodies, for the crown had only a small paid centralised bureaucracy. Relief of the poor became a foremost priority of this legislation. All this gave immense local power to the gentry.

However, the chief secular figure in the counties was the Lord Lieutenant, a politically reliable nobleman who replaced the sheriff, whose office became more ceremonial than practical. He was the monarch's representative and an important link between the counties and the court. He was also a key military figure, for he was responsible for the militia, the country's military force for home defence.

Population rapidly increased, from 2.25 million in 1526 to 4.1 million in 1603 – a large increase indeed, which led to strain on resources, price rises and an increase in poverty in the late sixteenth century. Yet most survived plague and war and by 1700, England's population stood at 5 million. This was still a rural society, with few towns of any significant size outside London, and communication was still basic.

Britain was becoming a united political entity in these centuries. England and Wales were formally joined in 1536, following the medieval dynastic link. England and Scotland shared a monarch from 1603, and in 1707, the Act of Union brought Scotland's existence as an independent political entity to an end. Successful wars resulted, by 1713, in Britain being recognised as one of the great powers of Europe as well as one of the world's leading maritime and colonial nations.

Hanoverian England, 1714–1837

The Elector of Hanover became George I in 1714. There was a question over his dynasty's survival in the face of threats from the exiled Stuarts. This led to major rebellions in both England and Scotland in 1715, but these were defeated within months. Except for the Jacobite rebellion of 1745, the country then enjoyed internal peace, which had not been the case in the previous century.

Major changes were occurring in society and economy, too. The 'Agricultural Revolution' accelerated change in the rural economy, with increasing amounts of arable land being enclosed by Acts of Parliament, and thus changing the face of the countryside forever. Farmers began to experiment with innovative methods of growing crops, resulting in higher yields. Elsewhere, industrial growth was being seen, especially in Lancashire, the West Riding of Yorkshire and in the Midlands, as industry became less concentrated on small-scale operations and began to be big business as factories were first created. However these developments should not be exaggerated as they took decades to become widespread.

Communication also underwent a lengthy revolution in the Georgian period, and this facilitated industrial growth, too. Roads were improved by turnpike trusts and so travel was quicker. Canals were dug in the latter half of the eighteenth century, thus easing the transportation of goods. Finally, just as this era was ending, steam power was harnessed to bring about the world's first railways. All these developments assisted in the process known to historians as the Industrial Revolution which was transforming Britain into the 'Workshop of the World' and thus bringing the modern age. The textile industry was the most important, with cotton becoming dominant by 1810. Coal and iron production also soared. Better techniques and inventions led to this.

Population increased, from about 5 million in 1700 to 8.3 million a century later and then to 13.1 million in 1831. London's population topped 1 million. Death rates were falling and birth rates rose. Yet in 1801, only 30 per cent of the population lived in towns, and most of these in towns with less than 10,000 people. Most of these towns were not industrialised, but maritime or dockyard towns, or regional centres. From 1835 many towns, such as Manchester and Halifax, became self-governing due to the Municipal Corporations Act of 1835.

Politically and constitutionally, the authority of Parliament gradually rose relative to that of the crown. Royal patronage declined in the later eighteenth century. Under George IV the prestige of the monarchy declined, too. The Reform Act of 1832 led to a redistribution of seats as well as an increase in the electorate – the first such changes to the constitution since the experiments of the Commonwealth. Political parties began to become more recognisable, with the Whigs and Tories being more than abusive labels to the factions of the late seventeenth century. New towns became constituencies in their own right. Radicalism emerged as a political force in the 1760s, and continued as a major extra-parliamentary force from thereon, partly aided by the growth of national and local newspapers.

There were several forms of Protestantism in the England of 1714, and their number grew in the century. The Wesley brothers founded Methodism which became the largest nonconformist grouping. Despite popular fears about Catholicism, the decline of Jacobitism as a political danger eventually led to anti-Catholic legislation being repealed, so that by the end of the eighteenth century Catholics could worship in peace and Catholic priests no longer feared legal prosecution. This led to a reduction in the influence of the established Anglican Church, yet this institution remained a powerful force into the nineteenth century.

Much remained the same. The counties continued to be ruled by the quarter sessions. However, central government grew in power relative to them, with the creation of the New Poor Law in 1834, which led to a decline in the administrative importance of the parishes. In 1833 the first government educational grant was made and in 1829 the Metropolitan Police was formed. The old order was changing, but at an evolutionary pace.

Victorian and Edwardian England, 1837–1914

Most of the changes in the later nineteenth century had their origins in the Hanoverian era. Yet they were greatly accelerated in the subsequent decades. Generally speaking, the powers of the state grew at a rate unimagined in the eighteenth century, both at the level of central and local government. The power of the established church, in some ways, was in decline, though this should not be exaggerated as church building and church schools were very much in evidence. A

Railways in the 1830s. (Author)

recommended website for this period is www.victorianweb.org/history/sochistov.html.

At the centre, the formal power of the monarchy was in decline, though under Queen Victoria, its prestige and influence soared following its disrepute under her immediate predecessors. Although Parliament was dominated by the gentry and nobility, as ever, the electorate rose following the Reform Acts of 1867 and 1885. Few householders now lacked the vote and in local elections, female householders were enfranchised by 1890. The party political system became more formalised, with the transformation of the Whigs into the Liberals and the Tories to the Conservatives. There was even a small party dedicated to the working classes by 1914: the Labour Party.

Locally, the parish became less important. Shorn of its poor law responsibilities, it began to lose its other powers. Legislation led to a number of 'boards' being set up in order to deal with specific problems, such as lighting, paving, health, burials and other matters of social importance. Quarter sessions, too, lost its administrative functions following the county councils being created after the 1888 Local Government Act. These new councils became the top tier of local government. Rural and urban district councils were an attempt in 1894 to pull together the different local government boards which had existed for some decades.

From 1833, the government took an increasingly interventionist role in education, too. From 1870 to 1902 the school boards had the power to raise money in order to build and run schools where the existing educational provision was thought to be lacking. Education at an elementary level did not become compulsory until 1880; by 1902 it was compulsory till the age of 12. District councils began to run schools from 1902. Universities began to grow in number, being established at Durham, London and Manchester amongst other cities.

The church lost its power over wills in 1858 and secular authorities took over; it lost its dominance over the universities, too. Although the Anglican Church was the state church by law established, Catholicism and nonconformity, no longer shackled by penal laws, established chapels throughout the country. Many Anglican churches were built in order to cater for the increased populations, especially in the expanding towns and cities. The parish and diocesan structure changed, with new parishes and dioceses being carved out of established ones in order to adjust to the changes in population.

Population increases in the period 1841–1901 were phenomenal, rising proportionately at a higher rate than at any time before or since; the population reached 30 million by 1901. Birth rates were as high as ever, but death rates were falling as epidemics had been eliminated and the standard of living increased. This led to great rises in the country's urban population whilst more ancient cities such as York and Cambridge were left behind. One manifestation of these population changes was an ever more sophisticated and detailed record of capturing the information by use of the census; another was the creation of a national system of civil registration of births, marriages and deaths.

England's industrial might soared. The Great Exhibition of 1851 in Hyde Park was an example to the world of that dominance. Internal trade was assisted by the great boom in railway building which took place throughout the century. Meanwhile the country became increasingly urban, educated and secular.

The Crystal Palace. (Paul Lang)

Modern England, 1914–2014

The general peace of the Victorian age was shattered by the two World Wars of the twentieth century, though Britain emerged victorious from both, at a severe cost in lives and treasure. Domestically, these wars led to wide-ranging social, political and economic changes.

England's population continued to rise, though at a lesser rate than it had in the nineteenth century (reaching 53 million by 2011). One powerful agent for population growth after 1945 was a great increase in overseas immigration; initially chiefly from Britain's colonial and former colonial possessions, but later from the continent of Europe, overtaking the numbers of people from Ireland who were the longer established immigrants. New faiths have been established as diverse communities have been created.

Politically, more and more people were enfranchised; in 1918 women over 30 and all men of 21 and above; in 1928 all adults aged 21 or more; in 1969 all aged 18 or older. The party system, in the 1920s, saw the decline of the Liberal Party as the Labour Party rose to be the rival party to the Conservatives in a two-party system. Smaller parties also emerged: Fascists, Communists, and later, the Green Party and UKIP. Central government increased its powers dramatically after 1945 when part of heavy industry, transport and health care was nationalised. The government became a very significant employer of labour and, to meet this, taxation and borrowing rose to levels previously unimaginable in peacetime. Since 1979 the role of the state has been reduced, but it remains a dominant force in society and the economy.

Local government has also changed considerably in the late twentieth century. Earlier in the century, additional powers were given to the district and county councils, including secondary education when it emerged in the 1920s and was expanded after 1944. Structurally the major changes occurred in 1965 for London and its environs and 1974 elsewhere. Some counties were abolished for administrative purposes and new metropolitan districts established. Middlesex was wiped from the map in 1965; the three Yorkshire ridings, Huntingdonshire and Rutland likewise in 1974, and six urban areas became metropolitan districts (these metropolitan districts were abolished in 1986), Liverpool and London for instance. New counties such as Avon, Cleveland and Humberside came into existence (abolished in the 1990s). More alterations occurred in the 1990s; Berkshire was abolished, but Rutland and East Yorkshire restored.

Britons became more educated, with rising minimum school-leaving ages and an increasing proportion going onto what had been the preserve of the minority, higher education, as the number of universities rose and those already existing expanded dramatically. Corporal punishment was abolished in the 1980s and, at state level, formal academic distinctions were reduced, but private schools continued to coexist with those of the state sector.

Employment radically altered in the last century. Work in the heavy industries of coal and steel declined rapidly in the late twentieth century as a result of government policy and mechanisation. Domestic service was another industry which contracted dramatically. In their stead, service industries increased. The workplace became far more open to women, too.

Over the centuries, England and its people have changed immensely. Yet the basic unit of the monarchical state, with a strong central government and local government at county or city level has endured, though in an altered format. Most communities have similarities as well as differences and their histories are far from homogeneous. The lack of major military operations on the mainland for centuries has assured that the survival of the materials for their histories has been at a far higher rate than less fortunate nations. It is to these that we now turn.

There are several websites which can help anyone beginning in local history; www.local-history.co.uk/getting started.html is probably the best to begin with; and useful resources can be found at www.nationalarchives.gov.uk/records/looking-for-place and www.national archives.gov.uk/records/atoz.

Chapter 2

BOOKS AND JOURNALS

The written word is the obvious, and easiest, place to start when exploring local history, if only to see what has already been written on the subject. Local history books have been written for centuries and are very variable in quality. These books will certainly not mention your ancestor by name unless they played a particularly prominent part in the development of the locality in question. However, they do provide information about how a place changed over time, who the major personalities were and the significant events that occurred there; or at least those selected by the author for inclusion. Unless a book is extremely large or the district chosen is very small, then the author must choose very carefully what he is to include and their priorities may not be the same as all their readers. It is well worth reading some or preferably all of the books written about a locality that your ancestors lived in.

Books are secondary sources; the majority were not written at the time of the events that the author is describing. They are therefore a synthesis and a selection of information chosen by the author. Often they indicate what is known about a topic but it is not the entirety of the potential information. They should be used as guides but not as definitive.

The collections of books held in local studies centres will vary considerably; some may not be books proper, but journals. The books may well date from the seventeenth century to the early twenty-first. Not all may be books as we often think of them, i.e. mass-produced by a publisher and then sold in local shops, but may be unpublished theses, typescripts or even manuscripts.

The advantage of published books is that they will have been read by more than one person and revised accordingly. The author may well have asked friends/colleagues and family to have read through the work for readability and grammar as well as factual content. The editor of the

Hanwell Library, 1905. (Paul Lang)

company will also have employed someone to have read it and they will have queried anything which looks 'odd' for whatever reason. The author will then have revised the text accordingly.

Books gathered together in a record office will include books specifically about the towns and villages that make up that office's jurisdiction. These are straightforward enough; clearly the ones relating to places associated with one's ancestors should be consulted. There will also be far more specific books. These may include books on particular schools, churches, businesses and other institutions which have existed in that locality. These are only of obvious use if one's ancestors had some connection with that place. Likewise there will probably be books about a district's transport or the locality during a time of conflict (especially the World Wars). These may be of no interest at all; but if your ancestors lived through the troubled times chronicled therein or if they were employed in the transport industry, then these books will provide background information about their lives. Some books may attempt a history of the whole county in which your ancestors lived. Books on a locality's famous people, or published memoirs/diaries and letters by former inhabitants may be of use, especially if your ancestors were connected to them, perhaps by way of employment or living in the same place at the same time as they did, so even if there is not any direct reference to them, the books may provide valuable context.

Some aspects of local history are relatively obscure and are the product of the interests of a local historian. Writings on these may well never have been meant for a wide audience or may not have been deemed of sufficient commercial worth for a publisher to be interested in them. Although Dr Johnson once wrote 'No man but a blockhead ever wrote except for money', this is not a sentiment often cited by local historians for whom there is more to writing than making a profit.

Library of Ealing and Notting Hill Girls' School. (Paul Lang)

Local history libraries often contain a number of typescripts or even manuscripts (the widespread use of computers has now thankfully made the latter relatively few) written by local historians. There is no qualification needed to be a local historian (local newspapers often use the term most indiscriminately). Some may be barely educated enthusiasts; others may be retired academics well used to research and writing. This is not to say that the products of the former will necessarily be inferior to those of the latter, of course. Local historians will often focus on a particular topic – I have met individuals whose interests include park railings, municipal toilets, clay pipes and bricks. The majority of unpublished works will not be of interest to all family historians but some will be. If your ancestor was employed in the clay pipe or brick works or as a parks or lavatory employee, those just mentioned are of obvious interest.

Don't forget that out-of-copyright books (mostly those published up to the early twentieth century) are often available online either for free, or hard copy can be bought fairly cheaply as they are print on demand books. If you are searching for such a book, do try searching for it online first.

We should also remember the products of academia which do not appear in journals or as books. In fact most academic theses, both undergraduate and postgraduate, will not be published. These theses are, or should be, the products of original research, written to satisfy the needs of a degree course, or far more substantial and rigorous (and larger), a doctoral thesis. Many cover national or international history (often political or military) but some will cover local history, often connected to a wider topic, for example, witchcraft in seventeenth-century Essex or Jacobitism in the northeast of England.

Other important parts of all these written works are the bibliography and the less common (except in academic theses) footnotes. As with indexes, these vary considerably in their being comprehensive. But they should at least provide a guide to suggested further reading, to primary as well as secondary sources, and these could lead onto other relevant sources of information.

One snag to be careful about when consulting books about local history is the prevalence of urban myth. Information in antiquarian histories is not always sourced, for example, and some authors have uncritically copied from these. Thus stories of doubtful provenance are repeated and gain credence by repetition and so become accepted as fact. That history does not repeat itself but 'historians' do is a dictum worth remembering. These tales often revolve around a famous or notorious character or about dramatic events such as plague and war or ghosts. For instance, a commonly believed story is that the Earl of

Chained Library, Lingfield Church. (Paul Lang)

Derwentwater, a Jacobite nobleman beheaded in 1716 for rebellion, was buried in Acton, Middlesex (there was a Derwentwater House there and there is still an obelisk to his memory in the park). In fact the peer never set foot in the place, alive or dead, and both house and obelisk postdate his death by over a century. It is a good story but alas, untrue, so as Indiana Jones is warned in the third film, 'Trust no one'. He fails to heed this excellent advice, but the historian must be wary. Only trust material which is backed up by evidence; if it sounds fantastic, it usually is.

Other books were published at the time of the events they describe, for example, the annual reports of the Medical Officer of Health. This post was required by law from the nineteenth to the twentieth centuries and was a local government appointment of a qualified medical professional, initially at a time when public health was seen as imperative by the government. Each year they had to produce a report, often 20–30 pages long, for the local authority in question. This would cover all the topics which might have an influence on the locality's health, from food standards, gypsy encampments, housing, schooling, pollution in the air or water and even comments on public transport and on aspects of the World Wars. There are statistical tables of deaths in the locality for the previous year, listing how many people (divided by sex) have died and from what cause. Causes are broken down by types of disease/ailment, as well as accidents, suicides, murders and, in wartime, death by enemy action. These are especially worth checking for the years in which your ancestors died in order to see how commonplace (or not) was the cause of your ancestors' deaths. If it was a death from a disease that was prevalent at that time and in that place, then the medical officer would almost certainly comment upon it elsewhere in his report and perhaps mention what steps were being taken to tackle its causes. Many such reports for London from 1848 to 1972 are available online at the Wellcome Institute for the History of Medicine, at http://wellcomelibrary.org/moh /reports. They can be searched by keyword (e.g. street or disease), year and borough.

One example is the Annual Report for the Local Board of Acton for 1888. We learn that the birth rate was 33.1 and death rate was 13.9, both per 1,000 residents. However, infant mortality was high; of 306 deaths, 113 were under one year (these are also given by street; nine babies died on Acton Green) and 155 under 5. Eleven deaths were by violence

20

(10 accidents, one suicide) and figures give deaths from a variety of diseases and other ailments. There is also a discussion of the various causes of deaths.

Journals are akin to magazines, and are produced by organisations; commercial, charitable, scholarly, clubs, civic, political and religious being the major categories. They are designed primarily for their members and are not always available commercially at time of release. They will tend to represent the official views of that organisation, though there is not always a 'party line' to be adhered to. They tend to date from the nineteenth century onwards, but most will be from the twentieth century, and still exist, often in electronic format in more recent times. They appear at regular intervals, some monthly, some quarterly and some annually.

The obvious run of journals to be found are those of historical/ antiquarian/archaeological societies which have a geographical connection to the district in which the library or record office is located. For instance, *Archaelogia Aeliana*, which has covered Northumberland historical topics since the early nineteenth century, should be found at Newcastle Central Library, at the City Archives and at the county record office. Clearly it would not be found on the shelves of the Centre for Kentish Studies at Maidstone (that would be *Archaeolgia Cantiana*). However, most of these county journals will be located at the National Archives Library and the British Library.

In the nineteenth century, gentlemen and clergy who were interested in their county's past began to meet regularly and discuss their mutual interests. Members would give talks to their fellows at meetings based on their recent researches and discoveries. Often these concerned artefacts dug up from the ground. Archives also provided material for these 'papers' and these talks would appear, often in modified forms, in these journals, so the fruits of research would be preserved for posterity.

The articles published are myriad indeed and limited only to the interests of members. They include local transport, former inhabitants and organisations. They may include reminiscences of former inhabitants. For example, the Halifax Antiquarian Society journal for 2013 had articles about Yorkshire Luddism, music at the parish church in Victorian times, the co-operative movement, the local newspaper and a locally born serial killer. Those writing the articles are often people

Transactions of the Halifax Antiquarian Society, *2013. (Author)*

engaged in historical research as students and teachers, or are retired people with an interest in local history.

Looking at over 100 volumes on shelves is often a daunting prospect and often an uninviting one. However, many have been indexed, often a number of a volumes at a time, and so searching for particular topics is straightforward. Some of these volumes and indexes are available online.

Allied to these volumes are those of record societies, often originating from the same time and existing in the same quantity, which aim to reproduce documents relevant to the county's history. The Chetham Society, covering Cheshire and Lancashire, and the Surtees Society, covering Durham and Northumberland, are two examples of such which date from the mid-nineteenth century. These volumes reproduce memoirs, diaries and letters from individuals in the county's history. Or they can be medieval accounts or trial records or the minutes of county or corporate government, churchwardens' accounts and so forth. The Sussex Record Society has had volumes published on the printed maps of the county, 1575–1900, cellarers' rolls of Battle Abbey, 1275–1513, Lewes Town Books, 1542–1901 (3 volumes), Sussex wills up to 1560 (4 volumes), correspondence of the Dukes of Newcastle and Richmond, 1725–50 and Acts of the Dean and Chapter of Chichester, 1545–1642. They are often indexed by name and topics, so searching for a particular subject is straightforward.

A journal which should be read by all those interested in local history is *The Local Historian*, which began life in 1952 as *The Amateur Historian*. Most local studies libraries keep complete runs of this journal. Each issue contains a small number of articles about topics dealing with particular issues of interest to local historians. The journal also includes reviews of local history books and related material.

Many journals are not primarily historical in origin or purpose, but have now become so. These were for the membership of organisations. They can vary considerably in interest to those who are not members but whose ancestors were. Parish magazines were produced by churches once they had largely literate congregations in the late nineteenth century. They were, and are, produced monthly. There will be usually an address by the vicar, often on spiritual or local issues, which can be of great interest. Just as significant is contemporary information about church societies, upcoming events and lists of church voluntary workers (churchwardens, Sunday School teachers and so on). In the past, and to a lesser extent now, churches run social and sporting groups such as youth clubs, mothers' meetings and football clubs. Of less interest are short stories, which were a regular staple of magazines and newspapers, but even they give a flavour of the type of fiction that your ancestor may have read.

School magazines often survive, especially for grammar and public schools, sometimes published twice or thrice per annum. If your ancestor attended the school, these are of obvious interest in case they are mentioned therein or if they wrote an article, poem or story. It is usually only the minority who win prizes or are members of the sports teams or who write articles/poetry for inclusion or who hold positions of responsibility (as a club captain or as a prefect for example). However, for the minority named as well as the majority who are not, these are an excellent source for the history of the school when your ancestor attended it. They help show what the school's values were and the events which took place there. They may detail fund-raising activity and the school's reaction to momentous events such as the Armistice of 1918. Their limitation is that they will not dwell on or even hint at activities at the school which show it in a bad light, such as disobedience or inept teaching (other records such as school log books and punishment books may be helpful here). If the school still exists, contacting the school librarian if there is one, or else the headteacher, is probably the best method of access, but local studies libraries may well hold copies. The British Library is another source, especially for well-known schools, such as Wakefield Grammar School. Former pupils and staff may have kept some. However, in most cases, magazines only survive for a few years and many schools did not create them.

Student magazines often exist for further education colleges and universities and can certainly provide an alternative view to the more official publications. Produced by students for students they can often suggest that the students are workshy and obsessed with drink and sex, or/and are stridently extremist politically speaking. However, social and political concerns among students are often featured (e.g. safety on campus) and so provide a counterpoise, and activities run by the student union also appear. Letters by individual students often give diverse views, too.

Work-based journals are often created by large organisations with hundreds or thousands of employees. These are often the official mouthpieces of the employer, and, as with the school magazines, are unlikely to feature controversial activity or discordant views. Yet if your ancestor was employed in this organisation, they are of clear value, if one always bears in mind the bias. There will be reports on the firm's progress towards meeting its goals in production and profit. Training courses will be mentioned. Employees who excel will be feted. Retiring employees may also feature. Social events will be reported. In the past, firms often provided sports and social clubs to an extent hard to imagine now, as well as an annual dinner/Christmas party. These often feature, along with pictures of happy employees. There may also be articles about the company's history. Trade unions may also produce publications which should be viewed in order to see a different, though no less biased, view of the firm and its employees.

Voluntary organisations also create journals, as do social groups or residents' associations of the twentieth century and beyond. If your ancestor was a member of this club or lived in the locality covered by the residents' association, they should be of interest. The editor is tasked by the club committee to find enough material to fill the magazine. This will usually include a record of the committee meetings in varied detail, a letter by the editor covering an important contemporary topic; perhaps a campaign or perhaps a commentary on the club successes or otherwise. There will probably be some advertising by local firms and then articles by other members or others whose arm the editor has been able to successfully twist. Sports and other clubs will list match fixtures and results. Forthcoming social events will be listed, and later, their results (who won the quiz or darts match for example). Not all clubs produce these and not all survive, but where they do they can provide a unique insight into an aspect of your ancestor's life or the concerns of the neighbourhood in the case of a residents' association campaigning for a better quality of local life.

There are also books which were not published as histories, but have become so over time. Counties and towns often had guide books written about them. These were often not intended for use by visitors, unless that town was on the tourist path – historic cities as Oxford and Winchester, or seaside towns, or capital cities – but by its inhabitants. These were often published by the council or the chamber of commerce and included considerable detail about the town as it then was (as well as adverts for private schools, shops and nursing homes). This would give information about the public authority running the place, about shops and industries, schools, transport, its history, leisure activities and would usually be well illustrated, include a map and local adverts. They were often published at intervals throughout the twentieth century but more recently tend to have been superseded by websites.

A similar form of publication are directories, whose heyday was the late nineteenth and early to mid-twentieth centuries. Their origin lay in the seventeenth century and some were still published in the 1970s by firms such as Pigot's, Kemp's and best known of all, Kelly's. The obvious genealogical use of these lays in searching lists of householders, shopkeepers and streets, but they do contain other information as well. Since each usually covers a town or county, there is often a great deal of general information about that place at the beginning. For county directories, which are usually divided by alphabetically by parish, each entry begins with a description of that parish and its amenities before listing tradesmen and a select list of its inhabitants. This information is similar to that given in borough or county guides, but directories were usually published annually, not at intervals of a few years as with the guides.

Neither of these two contemporary sources is designed as a candid and frank account of life in these districts. They were designed to show the attractions of a district to a potential newcomer, whether businessman or resident, as well as providing general information about those already in existence there. As with postcards, the less benign aspects of local life will not be mentioned. Newspapers may supply this defect.

CASE STUDY
From the Pigot's Directory of Middlesex, 1832.

HORNSEY, CROUCH END AND MUSWELL HILL
Hornsey is a village and parish, in the hundred of Ossultone, about 6 miles N.W. from the Standard, in Cornhill; agreeably situated in a vale, through which passes the new river, and is surrounded by hills commanding varied and beautiful views of London and the adjacent county. This place was anciently called Haringay; it has from a remote period belonged to the see of London, and the Bishops had formerly a park here. The parish comprises of the hamlets of CROUCH-END, MUSWELL HILL and STROUD GREEN, and greater part of the village of HIGHGATE. The places of worship are, the parish church of St. Mary, and a Baptist chapel at Crouch End: the church is of considerable antiquity, and in appearance peculiarly pleasing, being

nearly covered with ivy. The charities comprise a charity school upon the national plan for 50 boys, who receive clothing and another for 50 girls; also several benefactions for apprenticing boys, and for other charitable purposes. Here was situated the Hospital and Dairy farm belonging to the Knights of St. John of Jerusalem, the wells of which still sustain a reputation for medical efficacy; and at Muswell Hill was anciently a chapel, dedicated to the Virgin; much resorted to by pilgrims before the reformation; the principal attraction to visitors at this period, is the extensive landscape viewed from the summit, which embraces a delightful range of prospect over the metropolis, and the counties of Essex, Kent and Surrey. This neighbourhood is perhaps one of the most agreeable districts round London, and is inhabited by persons of the first respectability. The entire parish, contained in 1831, 4,856 inhabitants.

There then follows the times of the post and the post office, listings of gentry and clergy, the academies and schools, shopkeepers and traders, taverns and public houses, coaches and carriers.

The final type of contemporary publication which was never meant to be used for historical purposes is the electoral register. As with directories, the obvious use for family historians (looking up names) is not the only potential value of such books. Since the franchise expanded in the nineteenth and twentieth centuries, their value has increased as a form of recording, year by year, voters. They show a street or neighbourhood in a way that no other source after the most recently available census (currently 1911) can, as they are published annually (save for the years of the World Wars) and list all adults eligible to vote. It is possible to find, for example, when/if houses were subdivided into flats or how a district changed socially, perhaps because of immigration. In the former case, often builders foresaw that property would be resided in by the middle classes as single-household residences, but were unable to sell/let them to the envisaged market and so several working-class families lived there instead. Or perhaps the middle-class occupiers moved out and so the house was subdivided into flats for those on more modest incomes. Names of voters can indicate how the ethnic make up of a street altered over time; Polish names and Indian ones are easy to spot. However, those of West Indian residents are not always so (e.g. Beresford Brown, resident at 10 Rillington Place in the early 1950s, was a Jamaican), so care is evidently needed here. Electoral registers can also show the level of population density. Poorer districts tend to be far more densely populated than affluent ones, but children, ineligible to vote, are not recorded in these registers. However, looking at other families in the same street or neighbourhood as your family can show how an area has changed whilst your family were living there and might provide a clue to why they moved, if they did so.

British Museum. (Paul Lang)

Books are very accessible because, unlike many sources for local history, they have been published and survive in multiple copies. They are usually available on open access on the shelves of the library part of a record office (or in a bookshop), though rarer items may be locked away in cabinets. Some books can be ordered via inter-library loan. Others can be bought either second hand in bookshops or increasingly via online book shops, if they are not still in print (most have a limited shelf life in conventional bookshops unless they are best sellers).

Guides to counties or even the whole country, sometimes written by a traveller, are another form of book that can be interesting. They provide commentary about their experiences and about the places they visit. Sometimes these can be highly personal. This often makes them far more colourful, provided the reader is aware of possible bias. One famous late eighteenth-century traveller was retired soldier, Viscount Byng. Others include Celia Fiennes, writing at the end of the previous century, and Daniel Defoe's *Tour of the Whole Island*, first published in the 1720s. In the nineteenth and twentieth centuries books concerning whole counties were often published, with a few pages devoted to each town or village. Arthur Mee's *The King's England*, published in the 1930s, was a series of books covering all of England's counties, usually one per volume (three for Yorkshire). These books often concentrated on buildings of historical interest and on the journeys of the travellers, who also comment on the inadequacy of the accommodation they have to put up with. Some, such as Defoe's and Mee's were updated years after the deaths of their authors. The views in these books are inevitably dated, but this serves to give a flavour of the times in which they were written.

Byng's remarks on Brighton before it had become a popular resort can be cited as an example:

Brighton appear'd in a fashionable, unhappy bustle, with such a harpy set of painted harlots as to appear to me as bad as Bond Street in the spring, at three o'clock pm.

The Castle is reckon'd a good tavern, and so we found it completely; and most comfortably too, after our walking the Steyne, entering the booksellers' shops, sitting by the seaside and endeavouring to look like old residents: but not till we had been equipped by the masterly comb of Mr Stiles.

Nothing could be better than our dinner and the two bottles of claret and port that Wynn and I soon suck'd down: and then sighed for more wheatears after the many we had eaten dress'd to perfection. We then saw the magnificent assembly room here; and tho' we could not stay to see the play, we had a peep inside the Playhouse ... We did not leave Brighton till past seven o'clock; where is plenty of bad company, for elegant and modest people will not abide such a place!

Published diaries and letters are another great source – those for mid-eighteenth-century Sussex include those written by Thomas Turner and Sarah Hurst, and for Oxford and Norfolk in the same century, Parson Woodforde's are worth consulting as well as being an entertaining insight into the lives of the 'middling people', just as Pepys's and Evelyn's are for seventeenth-century London.

Books are the most accessible format in which to find information about local history. Depending on the amount of time and energy you have you may be content to read a selection of what is available. They vary considerably in value, depending on the author's skill in both research and in writing. Yet as a first port of call for the history of a locality or facets of it, they are hard to ignore, if only because they lead to other sources. Yet there are many more sources to explore as we shall see.

Chapter 3

PHOTOGRAPHS AND ILLUSTRATIONS

A picture is famously worth a thousand words, but some are more valuable than others. Documents and the written word will hopefully conjure up a mental picture, but this has to be informed by imagination (sometimes a dangerous matter for anyone interested in history) as well. Physical pictures are even better, because imagination can be ruled out. They recreate a moment in time, otherwise lost forever.

We are all familiar with those old photographs of our family in the present and near past. The latter tend to include pictures of important family occasions, such as marriages, educational achievement, new babies and school classes. They might also include photographs taken for special events such as military service or sporting success. If we are lucky we will know who the people in the photographs are, or their names will have been written on the back, and hopefully we have an idea of when and where they were taken. Unnamed and undated photographs of people in the past are the most frustrating of all. However, fashions of the sitters, especially if female, can help give an approximate date. Yet apart from these valuable photographs, there are others.

The digitalisation of photographs has proved irresistible for some of those institutions which hold them in quantity. This is not surprising because they are attractive and interesting and lend themselves to being easily searched.

There are a number of general websites dedicated to British photographs; www.oldaerialphotos.com gives bird's eye views. Others include www.cyndislist.com.photos and www.imagesofengland.org.uk. Collections of regional photographs can be found at www. collage.cityoflondon.gov.uk for London, www.ideal-homes.org.uk for six southeast London boroughs, www.westsussexpast.org.uk/pictures, www.picturethepast.org.uk for the northeast of England, www. leodis.net for Leeds, www.picturesheffield.com, www.chesterimage bank.org.uk and www.buryimagebank.org.uk. Photographs of London's transport can be seen at www.ltmcollection.org/photos; Aylesbury prisoners at www.buckscc.gov.uk/leisure-and-culture/centre-for-buckinghamshire-studies/online-resources/victorian-prisoners; those of 8,000 churches can be seen at www.genuki.org.uk/big/churchdb. And there are many more, of all sizes.

It is now time to examine the history of photographs and photography to learn their significance and limitations for family history purposes. It was a process invented in France and England in the early nineteenth century and photographs began to be taken in the 1840s and 1850s. Initially they were few in number. Most were taken by professional photographers who were often chemists and set up in business in towns and cities in the nineteenth century. They would take photographs of individuals, couples and families for special occasions, and working-class as well as middle-class people were photographed (some of Jack the Ripper's victims were photographed with their husbands before their decline into poverty and prostitution). Pictures were also taken of war scenes in the Crimea and in America in the 1850s and 1860s.

But photographers also took pictures of landscapes, both rural and urban. Few exist for the 1840s, with rather more in the 1850s. By the 1870s and 1880s they became increasingly common. These are valuable sources for family history. Photographs were taken for many reasons. Newspapers, especially in the twentieth century, often commissioned photographs. They might include pictures of important events such as the reading of the town's charter, a jubilee or coronation celebration, severe weather or events on the Home Front during the World Wars. Other organisations would do likewise.

Photographers began to set up business in large towns and cities and travelling photographers visited villages. Between 1842 and 1912 there were 633 in Birmingham. Some travelled throughout the country, such as Francis Frith, and built up extensive collections, but others did not stray far from their home town or county and so most of the early photographs of a particular place are the products of a handful of photographers.

A range of photographs of the same place over decades is a

Family photograph at Calvados, Ealing. (Paul Lang)

photographic history of the place. It will show buildings long gone, those hugely altered and those which remain. There will be buildings which were new at the time of the earlier pictures and which were subsequently demolished. Changes in transport, from horse-drawn to combustion engine and from steam trains to diesel, and from electric trams to trolley buses to motor buses, will be evident. Changes in fashion are also noticeable. Crowd scenes are also informative and were often taken in the hope that those pictured would buy them or that the scene was of a sufficiently important event that people would buy them as souvenirs. These might include fairs, coronation or jubilee celebrations, market days, recruitment drives and so on. Adverts are often shown on photographs, mostly words, unlike today. Litter rarely appears on these scenes and streets often seem less congested.

Technology changed throughout the history of photography. The first photographs were daguerreotypes, which required considerable immobility on the part of the subject matter. William Fox Talbot invented the paper negative in 1838–41 and this allowed shorter exposures. The wet plate of the 1850s did even more to usher in an army of photographers who could be mobile, with a dark room in their wagon of equipment. By the 1880s there were hand-held cameras and dry plates, so photography was now also in the realm of the wealthy amateur photographer.

Sometimes photographic surveys were taken of particular districts at a given year in time. The Croydon Natural History Society made a photographic record of Surrey in the first half of the twentieth century. There was a photographic survey of Horsham in the 1950s. There were also surveys of Caterham and Lambeth in the 1960s. All these soon acquired historical significance.

Hoddesdon High Street, Hertfordshire, 1981. (Mrs Bignell)

The difficulty with photographs is that they may be undated. They may show unusual or quaint people or places, rather than commonplace ones, and may well be untypical of the time and place and therefore less useful as a reliable historical source. Locations of photographs maybe unknown if there is nothing recognisable or identifiable using other sources. Pictures of side streets and fields often fall into this category. Photographs can be wrongly labelled in both books of old photographs and even within local studies collections; archivists and local history librarians cannot be expected to know every building past and present within their jurisdiction.

Clues to dating and locating the whereabouts of particular pictures exist therein. Transport shown in a picture can help to date it, and, if the picture shows a tram or bus, then this will narrow down the location because they will run only on specific routes, usually the principal roads of a town or city. Costumes worn by people in the picture, especially if female, can also help date the picture, as the era of the fashions can be ascertained. If there are shops in the picture, reference to relevant street directories can both locate and help date the picture. If a postcard, the stamp and date mark on the reverse should also narrow down the date of the picture, but bear in mind that a postcard with a date stamp of 1906 may well have been taken up to several years earlier. However, if the scene is purely residential or shows a nondescript garden or open space, identifying the picture is far more difficult and may be an impossibility

Initially photographs were only taken by professional photographers and wealthy amateurs. Equipment was expensive and developing pictures was time consuming. It was not until the early to mid-twentieth century that photography became a mass pursuit.

One excellent source of photographs from the past are postcards, about three inches by five in size and usually landscape. Initially these dated from about 1870 in England, following their invention in Austria in the previous year, but were blank on both sides (one for the address and one for the message) and were a cheap and reliable form of communication useful in a society when universal education had led to increased literacy. However, by the 1890s illustrations began to appear on them, but only on half of one side (the other half was blank for the message) and so pictures and messages were restricted.

Barnstaple High Street. (Paul Lang)

In 1902, the Post Office allowed the picture to appear on all of one side of the card, making the postcard a mini work of art. Photographers, apart from taking studio photographs, began to photograph local scenes, such as prominent buildings (churches, town halls, historic places, schools) and attractive places such as bridges, rivers, woods, parks and commons. But they also took pictures of residential streets as well as shopping streets (these often appeared in limited runs and were sold from door to door). These featured people and transport as well. Sometimes disasters were depicted: fires of buildings or air raids in the First World War. Their heyday was about 1900–20. Some were black and white, some were sepia and some were hand coloured. Their main drawback is that they are very selective and some views are very rare indeed; small side streets, slums and factories will generally not appear. This is because these pictures were not meant as historical records but as attractive pictures.

People would use postcards as a popular form of communication, as messages on their reverse attest; they were used to arrange meetings as well as to pass on news. The postal service was far more frequent in the early twentieth century, with numerous deliveries per day, compared to only one in the early twenty-first century. Postage was cheap; a half penny only before 1914. The industry boomed and companies from overseas also began making postcards of places in Britain; before 1914 there were several German photographers who did so.

As the twentieth century progressed, postcards became less popular due to higher postage charges, the increased number of cheap cameras and greater usage of the telephone. They became reduced to being of tourist attractions and postcards of 'ordinary' views became almost extinct by the middle of the century. It should also be noted that some postcards include the messages written by the sender and these often provide a fascinating insight into that writer's life and concerns.

Reverse message on postcard. (Paul Lang)

Postcards can be accessed in a number of ways. First, museums, libraries and record offices often sell reproductions of old postcards and these can be bought cheaply. Secondly, books showing reproductions of old postcards are fairly common. Thirdly, genuine old postcards can be bought, at varying prices, depending on both rarity and content (e.g. pictures of fire engines and fire stations are often rather expensive). They can be bought at postcard collectors' fairs as well as postcard shops. Or it is probably easier to look on eBay and type in the name of the place one is seeking and add 'postcard', to bring up thumbnail sketches of those which meet the category sought, together with price and details of seller. Some can be seen online, perhaps on a local history society's website.

Organisations often have photographs taken for the purpose of forwarding their own business aims. The acquisition or hoped-for acquisition of new land, property or equipment might be an occasion for photographs to be taken. Special events such as a presentation or an annual social event or party might be recorded for posterity, as might a retiring member of staff. The launch of a new project or its culmination might be another occasion for photography.

Newspapers in particular have been using photographs since the early twentieth century. Those which actually appear and are now viewed digitally, on microfilm or occasionally on paper, are usually of low quality. However, the originals, or good copies, sometimes survive, and are often are available in record offices. These will usually only be a sample of all the photographs ever taken by the said newspaper. They will usually be of people and of events, rather than places. Councils may have photographs of councillors and public buildings; churches may have pictures of major events in the life of the church's clergy, people and buildings.

Individuals also take photographs, and increasingly did so as the twentieth century progressed, when cameras became cheaper and easier to use. By the 1950s they were in reach of most people. Many pictures taken are of family and friends, especially on significant occasions and on holidays; some may be of other events and places. Most rarely reach a record office or library for public consultation and when/if offered would be heavily weeded.

The use of photographs is that they give a snapshot into the past, into buildings and localities which may no longer exist or if they do will probably be substantially different. Most collections will be mainly topographical, showing streets, shops, buildings, especially prominent or picturesque ones, landscapes and parks, from different time periods. Some may be of these places during or after unusual events, such as after a flood, or during a fire, or perhaps a man-made disaster, as with the aftermath of bombing in the Second World War. Large and prominent places will be more photographed than others; expect more pictures of a major shopping street and of a railway station and less, if any, of small residential streets. These photographs may well include people or transport appearing incidentally on them.

Collections of pictures can often be seen in local studies libraries. These include those of newsworthy people; visiting celebrities, local and national politicians, centenarians and others. These may be of less interest, unless your ancestor is among these. Perhaps of more interest are group photographs; of schoolchildren, local police, fire or ambulance personnel, or of sports teams. Not only is there a greater chance of an ancestor being present, but they give a little clue to people who your ancestor may have known or have seen. Events may have been photographed: a protest march or strike, or a carnival or other social, political or religious function. These will add colour and a further dimension to what is known about such events which your ancestor may have been witnessed or have been involved in. There might also be photographs of objects, from recycling bins, street lamps or even prototype tanks made by a local inventor.

Local studies libraries usually have thousands of photographs in their collections, dating from the later nineteenth century onwards. As with all such collections, they will vary in quantity considerably, depending on how successful they have been in collecting what has been taken. Certain subjects and time periods may predominate. They might have received a large deposit of photographs taken in the 1950s and 1960s by a local photographic society or from a newspaper in the 1970s. Conversely there may well be few photographs taken during the First World War or the mid-Victorian era.

There are also important national collections of photographs, too. The National Archives has a large collection of over 13,000 from 1920 onwards. The Guildhall Library in London has over 10,000 pictures of London from the 1850s onwards; mostly central London and the City, but also of what were outlying districts in Middlesex, too.

The largest single collection, however, is the English Heritage Archive at Swindon, once known as the National Monuments Record for England, focusing on architecture from 1859, with about 12 million items in the collection. There is also a substantial collection of aerial photographs, too, as well as drawings and plans of buildings and man-made structures, from country houses to coal mines. By 2015, over half a million of these can be viewed as thumb nail sketches online and over a million can be searched for by keyword online, too. Copies can be ordered electronically.

Given recent advances in technology and new funding streams, digitising picture collections has proved a popular option for many record offices and local studies collections (those held by Manchester Central Library and Leeds Local and Family Studies Library have been made available, for example). Some collections will be available on the organisation's website, though it is rare for all the collection to be there. Most of these online collections can be searched by keyword, so it should be fairly straightforward to locate what you wish to find without even visiting the place. Copies can usually be made, though a fee will be payable (if it is not for publication elsewhere, this should be moderate). If collections are not digitised, it is usually possible to take copies on site, depending on copyright issues (currently a photograph, as with any work of art, remains the copyright of the creator or their heirs until 75 years after the creator's death). Again, a fee may be payable.

Many photographs are in private hands. Postcard and photograph collectors have their own collections and whilst many are duplicates held elsewhere, some may well be unique. Postcard societies and collectors' clubs exist where the likeminded can meet and discuss their collections. They have talks or create books of their collections. One society is the West London Postcard Club, www.chiswickw4.com/community/wlpc.

As with all evidence, care must be taken when judging how representative photographs are of contemporary life. To help with this, the key question to ask is why the photograph has been taken and to consider the occasion. In some instances we can never know this, but in others we can usually make an educated guess. The camera may never lie, but the pictures it takes may be designed to give the viewer a certain impression that those responsible for the picture wish to give.

For instance a picture taken of slum dwellers appearing downcast and miserable may have been taken by a social reformer or one who advocates that measures be taken to improve the housing stock of that particular district. Dr Barnardo was accused of making impoverished orphans look even more wretched in order that they could be photographed in that state, together with a later photograph showing them to be smart, a tribute to the work in his homes, to be used as propaganda, encouraging donations. To show the same people having fun, e.g. children playing football or skipping, would not have the same impact. Likewise, a business will want to show contented employees working in hygienic conditions, especially if food is involved. This is not to say that these pictures have been faked or are unreal, but they may not be wholly representative of conditions which they are portraying.

Postcards and photographs can also be incorrectly labelled by either the photographer, who may not know the district well or may choose to label it incorrectly. Pictures in libraries and record offices may have been wrongly titled. There is also the temptation for a photographer to take pictures of extraordinary events or particularly picturesque scenes or costumes, e.g. villagers taking part in a medieval themed play in the 1920s rather than their being photographed in their ordinary clothes on their way to work.

Often photographs of what we want to see simply do not exist. Wartime censorship resulted in relatively few private photographs being taken then. Those that were were often commissioned by civil and military authorities, and if for public consumption, will tend to shy away from the more unpleasant aspects of conflicts. However, they often show bomb-damaged buildings and streets, civil defence workers, military activity and parades, street parties at the war's end and these are of obvious interest.

Paintings and Prints
Apart from photographs there are two other major sources of images held. Both cover the pre-photographic age. The first are prints, which, compared to photographs, are relatively few in number, but are often the only visual representation of places and people prior to the mid-nineteenth century. They tend to focus on significant people and places; churches and large houses rather than cottages, workshops or workhouses. Yet humbler dwelling places featuring in general views of

Painting of St Augustine's church, Broxbourne, 1999. (Author)

villages and towns can be the only visual representation of these places centuries ago. They will certainly be few in number, but are clearly better than nothing. Local repositories have collections, as do museums and art galleries. The National Gallery and National Portrait Gallery have substantial collections, which can be searched online. Prints are usually black and white or greyscale, but a few are coloured. Some appear in published works – older histories and *The Gentleman's Magazine*, for example.

The other visual source are paintings. Again, these are few in number because a great deal of time, talent and effort is needed to create such a work of art, whereas numerous photographs can be taken in the same time. Individuals and members of art groups often choose local views, though certain ones are very popular (e.g. a picturesque church is a more likely subject than a row of terraced houses). Paintings, of course, can be very variable in quality depending on the artist's skill and can potentially be rather subjective. Yet they are unique creations and are in colour, unlike photographs from the nineteenth and early to mid-twentieth centuries, and that gives them an additional dimension compared with other visual representations of the past. Again, the National Gallery and National Portrait Gallery have substantial collections. Paintings of local scenes are still being painted, often with varying degrees of expertise, but the views will almost certainly be contemporary and not (to us, at any rate), historical.

A recent project by the Public Catalogue Foundation is to scan and show oil paintings held by public institutions online. 'Public institutions' includes universities, libraries, record offices and museums. They can be seen on www.thepcf.org.uk and can be searched by keyword. Basic additional details (name of painting, artist, dates, size and location) are given and copies can be ordered. However, it is worth noting that most paintings are not oils and so this collection shows a small but significant number of paintings throughout the country, and it also enables increased access. Most are landscapes but some are of people and some of scenes overseas.

Generally speaking, pictures were created in abundance from the later nineteenth century and beyond. Apart from very significant people, places and events, pictures of other views and people are very rare for the periods prior to the late nineteenth century. For the twentieth century, the coverage is far better. It is very likely that you will be able to find pictures of the locations that your ancestors would have known and so provide an insight into their environments.

Chapter 4

MAPS AND PLANS

Maps are not an obvious source for family history. They concern places and not people (geography is about maps and history is about chaps as the old saying goes). They exist in great number, especially for the last two centuries. For local historians, maps are an essential research tool, especially when they exist in a series over a lengthy period of time, in order to trace the development of a district.

Medieval maps are very few indeed; the Mappa Mundi located at Hereford springs to mind. Nor are they very reliable. The first local map is of Inclesmoor, Yorkshire, made in the first decade of the fifteenth century. There were also some maps of towns, such as Bristol, made in this century. Very few maps were needed and in any case, the cartographic skill was lacking.

There are several websites devoted to maps: www.cyndislist. com/maps, www.mapseeker.co.uk/genealogy and www.visionofbritain. org.uk. A number for London can be found at www.collage.cityof london.gov.uk.

County Maps

County maps began to be made in the sixteenth century as part of the interest in topography and local history. Christopher Saxton (c.1542–1611) had maps of 34 counties created between 1574 and 1579 and these were engraved and printed by his master. They were published in *An Atlas of England and Wales* in 1579. These maps showed villages in their relation to one another for the first time. However, they did not depict roads between the marked settlements and were not to the same scale.

Shortly afterwards, John Norden (1548–1626) produced county maps, but this time they showed roads and distances and used a grid reference system, so the locating of particular towns and villages was made less difficult. They were produced in the early seventeenth century.

VII 13. The first printed map of the British Isles drawn by an Englishman, George Lily, in 1546. Published at Rome by Antonio Lafreri.

First printed map of British Isles, 1546. (Paul Lang)

He never completed his work; there were no maps of the Midlands and the northern counties. Only the maps of Middlesex and Hertfordshire were produced during his lifetime. Posthumous maps were of Cornwall, Essex, Hampshire, Surrey and Sussex. Details are sometimes suspect,

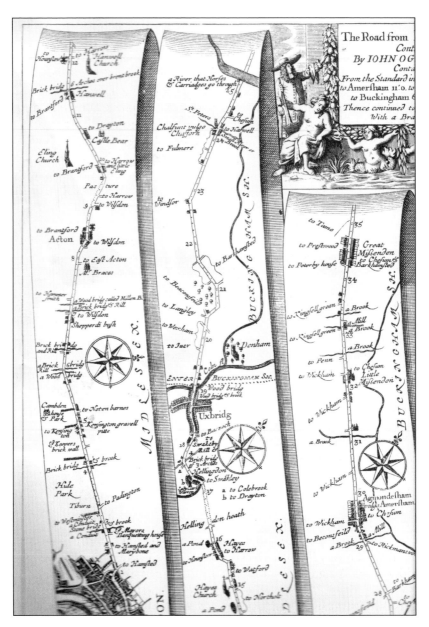

Extract from a John Ogilby map of 1675. (London Borough of Ealing)

though. Norden's and Saxton's maps were used as the basis of the maps in William Camden's *Britannia* of 1607.

John Ogilby's maps of major roads and settlements thereupon were produced a century later in a book of 100 plates and titled *Britannia* in 1675. They are on the scale of one inch to the mile. These were aimed at travellers and had counties reduced into strips showing principal coach routes and the settlements they passed through. Roads leading off the main routes were shown, together with the settlements they led to. He noted bridges which crossed rivers and what they were built of. An updated set of these maps was produced in the following century by Emmanuel Bowen, in his *Britannia Depicta* or *Ogilby Improv'd*. However, it is not always certain that Ogilby strayed from the main roads; for example, he depicts St Mary's church in Hanwell being to the west of the river Brent, which it is not, but from the road it would appear to be so because the bend of the river is not visible from there.

There were other eighteenth-century mapmakers in Britain. John Cary and Hermann Moll produced atlases of county maps. Cary paid particular attention to the accurate depiction of transport networks. John Rocque produced both town and county maps at this time, and is best known for his map of the districts ten miles around London as well as the city itself. It was reprinted several times. He also designed maps of Bristol, Exeter and Shrewsbury, all in the same decade. Rocque's maps have been criticised on account of errors of distance and direction compared to later and more accurate maps, but the tools at his disposal were rudimentary. Henry Beighton produced one of the best county maps of the century, but of only one county, Warwickshire, one of the first to be based on trigonometrical principles and was one inch to the mile in scale. County maps were still being produced in the nineteenth century.

Town and Village Maps
City and town (not village) maps began to be made in the sixteenth century. The very first was of Norwich, then one of the most important cities in the kingdom, by Dr William Cunningham in 1559. However, their quantity greatly expanded in the seventeenth century. John Speed was the first major mapmaker of such, including maps of a number of the county's principal towns as part of his series of county maps at the beginning of the seventeenth century. These were based on the earlier

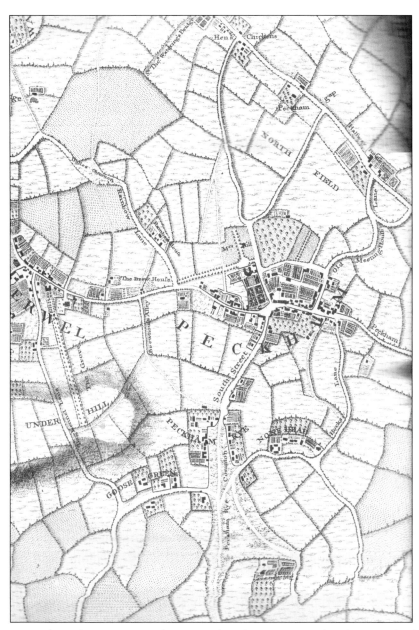

Extract from John Rocque map of environs of London, 1741–1745. (London Borough of Ealing)

maps by Saxton and Norden. They were often highly illustrated and attractive pieces of art. They often adorned the walls of the houses of the well to do, especially if their properties or names were depicted there. The maps were black and white, with the intention that they could be coloured by seller or buyer. Most of these towns had been surveyed by Speed himself. They can be viewed on www.lib.cam. ac.uk/deptserv/maps/speed.html. However, his maps were reproduced up to the next century and a half without any modifications, despite the changes that occurred in these towns in those decades.

Villages mostly remained unmapped. There was no demand to justify the expense of their production. However, in some villages, where there were a number of seats of the gentry and nobility, there might be a sufficient demand to lead to such, or there might have been a need by the parish for such a map, perhaps for rating purposes. Some were created and survive, but they are generally few in number.

Enclosure maps were made of agricultural land enclosed in the later eighteenth and early nineteenth centuries, and are often the first detailed maps of the parish. Enclosure commissioners had to have surveys undertaken to ascertain ownership of existing land and of rights over common land. Not all parishes were surveyed, however, and for some large parishes, mapping took years to complete. These maps are usually held at the county record office, and they should be accompanied by a schedule of landowners. These maps show the strip field system as well as land already enclosed and a second map showing the new arrangement of land in the said parish, though the former map, being of less practical and immediate use, may not always survive (more do so after 1830). Not all parishes had land enclosed (there are virtually none for Kent or Devon and only half of Northamptonshire was affected) and not all maps survive, but where they do they should not be overlooked. It has been estimated that 5,000 parishes had land enclosed. The associated paperwork is equally important. The Enclosure Award was drawn up to record the Commissioner's decisions about various matters, such as tenure, economics and topography.

A systematic survey of much of Britain was taken in the early nineteenth century (1836–51). This was the result of the Tithe Commutation Act of 1836 where tithes (taxes paid to the church on land) were converted to rents. This led to the tithes commissioners appointing surveyors to make large-scale maps showing, parish by parish, land and property within the said parish. They also made apportionments to accompany the maps and these list, per numbered plot, landowner, landholder, acreage, land usage (house, arable, pasture, commons and so forth) and payment to be made. Buildings are also shown and are sometimes coloured to denote different types. Field names are also given. These were the first reliable maps made of many parts of the country and the first detailed, national, survey. Yet, as with enclosure maps, they do not cover every parish in the country. Only about a quarter of Northamptonshire is covered, for example. But by and large they exist to a far greater degree than the enclosure maps. They can be located at the National Archives as well as at county record offices. Their scale is very variable and their accuracy is variable, too. Only about one-sixth of these maps are deemed first class for their accuracy, some are not even based on a survey but on earlier maps.

Ordnance Survey Maps

Perhaps the most important – and accurate – series of maps was initiated for military purposes. This was the Ordnance Survey. The creation of maps for military purposes began shortly after the defeat of the Jacobites at Culloden in 1746 and was restricted to Scotland. Another war led to the Board of Ordnance, a key department of state (in 1791), initiating the surveying of the south coast of Kent in case of invasion from France half a century later. These were to the scale of one inch to the mile and were published from 1801, the first being for Kent, and are known as the First Edition or Old Series, and in 1805–73, 110 sheets (mostly 36 by 24 inches in size) were published. The next maps were of the southern counties and by 1840 all the counties in England and Wales had been mapped south of Lancashire and northern Yorkshire. Clearly these were incapable of showing detailed maps of villages and towns, but are useful for showing geographical features, communications, the locations of settlements and their growth over time.

There were further editions of the one inch scale maps as time moved forward. Maps of northern England were produced between 1840 and 1872 and then maps for the whole country were revised from 1873 to 1898. Some of the second edition were coloured. Then there was a third edition to the same scale in the decade before 1914, producing 360 sheets of 12 by 18 inches in size. The fourth edition was published between 1918 and 1926 and there were further editions in

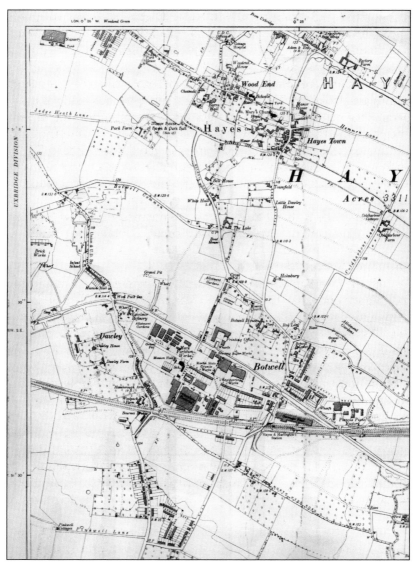

Extract from 1894 OS Map of Botwell, Middlesex (London Borough of Ealing)

later decades, though the fifth edition of the 1930s only included southern England as that series was discontinued. These maps were continually being amended to show any changes in local topography.

Larger scale OS maps were produced in the second half of the nineteenth century and these are of the greatest of value to family and local historians because they show a great deal of detail. They were produced at the scale of 6 and 25 inches to the mile from 1840 to 1900 and cover the whole country in 15,000 and 51,000 maps respectively by scale. The initial surveys undertaken between 1840 and 1854 were of Lancashire and Yorkshire and these were of the 6 inch scale. The first county to be mapped on the larger scale was Durham, which began in 1856. The rest of the country was so mapped in the next decade. There were further revisions made roughly every two decades (1890s, 1910s, 1930s). They showed streets, individual buildings (not numbered), with prominent buildings labelled, prominent features and street furniture. Ancient remains were often included on these maps. Natural features, streams, marshes, fields and hedges are depicted, as are quarries, gravel pits and pasture. Never before had such details been recorded. They also show boundaries of parishes and other jurisdictions which may not be evident by other means and may be long gone. The first edition sheets only show part of a single parish per map and leave the remainder of the sheet blank; so the adjoining sheet will be needed to show the adjoining parish (later editions showed portions of multiple parishes where applicable). Each map has a serial number, with the first two editions using the same grid and the third and fourth ones using another.

At the other end of the scale, for 400 towns and cities, there was, in the mid to late nineteenth centuries, a series of 1:500 scale maps, which is the most detailed to have been produced and shows minute details, down to each lamp post, fountains, pillar box, even garden paths. Rooms in large public buildings (such as workhouses) are often shown and labelled, and the number of seats in churches is noted on these maps. Nothing like it has been produced before or since. Most towns were only mapped once in this way, however.

After the Second World War there were new series, on a larger scale, of 1:1250 or 50 inches to the mile; these cannot be directly compared to their predecessors but, of course, show more detail. These also included house numbers, so making the task of identifying individual properties easy. They also show the elevations of selected points on each map above sea level. Those maps produced in the 1950s often show buildings which had been damaged by bombing in the war and had yet to be rebuilt (usually marked 'Ruin'). There was another revision in the 1970s and another in the 1990s. Few Ordnance Survey maps have been published in recent years, for they are now available digitally from the OS website www.ordsvy.gov.uk.

The great value of the OS maps are that they can be relied upon for accuracy, unlike the earlier plans. Their only slight failing is that, because of their detail, they are very sizeable and so several maps are needed to be able to view a town or a geographically scattered village. It is fairly easy to compare parts of the town for different years, but not its entirety, making a comprehensive comparison difficult.

The Ordnance Survey has also produced a number of historic maps of the country in the centuries up to the seventeenth, though concentrating on the centuries prior to the Norman Conquest. Since few people can confidently trace their ancestors prior to 1066, most of these will not be of direct value. However, there is one of Britain in the late seventeenth century, with a scale of an inch to 15 miles. Monastic Britain shows medieval Britain at a scale of an inch to 10 miles and provides ecclesiastical information.

Many Ordnance Survey maps (over 2,000 at time of writing) have been reproduced by the Alan Godfrey map company of Gateshead www.alangodfreymaps.co.uk. This is not comprehensive and focuses on the late nineteenth and early twentieth centuries. They also come with a survey of the particular district, often by a local historian, which adds extra value. It often includes extracts from a local directory, too, and is published in a short and easily portable format (which is not the case with full-scale copies or originals of OS maps), so tracing the places on the ground is relatively straightforward.

Care needs to be taken with maps as with any other historical source. First, there is a time lag, often of some years, between the time that the survey was made and the time that it was published. For instance a map of west London dated 1874 does not show streets which we know from rate books existed in 1869. Secondly some maps may not be wholly comprehensive in their depiction of geographical features. So we must take care and check with other available sources.

Other Maps
There are also other maps which were produced. The Charles Booth Poverty Map of what is now inner London is well known, though

perhaps not as much as it should be amongst family historians. It shows London streets, graded by wealth. Gold represents the wealthiest, with various gradings of red and blue shades to denote the middle and working classes. Lowest of all were those marked in black, showing streets inhabited by the semi-criminal and vicious. Do remember that these gradings were of a moment in time (1886–1903), and over the years streets may well have altered, being either gentrified or falling into the slum category. They can be viewed online at www.booth.lse.ac.uk.

Other one-off maps include those showing bomb damage in the Second World War. Local authorities commissioned such maps, often using 6 inch OS maps and then annotating them accordingly. These might show the dates when bombs fell and the type of bomb (oil bomb, high explosive, V1, V2 and others). Not all bodies created these and nor, if they did, do they all survive. But where they do they give a graphic portrayal of which parts of a town or city were worst hit, and when. Earlier military maps showing towns and their role in conflict were made following other warfare, including Preston after the battle there in 1715 and Carlisle after its sieges of 1745.

Archaeological surveys are often made when new buildings are erected. These result in a collection of maps for that particular site being drawn together, with details of any archaeological finds on the site and with other contextual information, all in one place.

In the first half of the twentieth century and beyond, slum clearance was a major policy for councils, replacing them with council houses or, after 1945, flats. These resulted in maps and plans of the new estates being drawn up. Local authorities and companies often had to commission plans when undertaking the building of new roads, new buildings and new housing estates. These resulted in detailed plans; for buildings these often included elevations as well as plans, often in great detail, showing windows, doors and other features. Plans of individual buildings and extensions to them sometimes exist, too. Drainage plans were an absolute imperative from the nineteenth century onwards, and all councils, often in their town planning departments rather than their archives, should hold them, perhaps microfilmed or scanned, for use. Plans of schemes never undertaken may also be held, giving an insight into an alternative future that was never to be. For example, in Ealing there is a depiction of a middle-class housing estate, with detached houses and neatly laid out streets and gardens, which was only partially realised.

Other new utilities also meant the creation of maps. These include canals, railways and improvements to docks. After 1794 these plans had to be deposited at what is now the Parliamentary Archives because they were needed to accompany the Private Act of Parliament which had authorised them. Local copies may be held at the appropriate county or borough record office.

Maps can pinpoint where an ancestor was baptised, married or buried, where their wife/husband's family lived, where they went to school, where they worked or where they enlisted in the armed forces or where they spent their leisure hours. You can trace how they probably travelled to these places which were important in their lives.

We should not neglect geological maps for geology played a crucial part in a district's history and the employment of many of its inhabitants. There have been a number of geological surveys, or rather revisions from the 1860s. Some are one inch to the mile; others are 6 inches to the mile, superimposed on OS maps. These maps are coloured in order to show the different types of soil, such as gravel, chalk, London clay, brickearth, alluvium and flood plain gravel. There are also comments on the maps, such as 'gravel formerly extensively dug over this area'. Comments about archaeological finds and the depth of earth are also sometimes noted.

Estate maps are another source. They can vary in scope a great deal. If the village where your ancestors lived was part of a large estate, as many were, then the land may well have been surveyed as part of the owner's attempt to learn exactly what he owned and how best to make use of it. They were also created when a sale was impending or to solve land disputes between neighbours. Or the plans may show individual farms and their lands. Only about a tenth cover an entire parish; some straddle several. They can date from as early as the sixteenth century up to the nineteenth, so are especially useful for they may be the oldest detailed map of part of a village or town. Field names are often given, as are footpaths, roads, common land, woods, but not necessarily what the land was used for. For the pre-enclosure era, patterns of strip farming should be shown here. Buildings, both domestic, ecclesiastical and industrial, also feature. Seventeenth- and eighteenth-century estate maps also showed industrial areas, such as the coal mines in Northumberland or the iron foundries in the Midlands. Livery companies and other institutions commissioned building projects in towns and so had maps of their intended developments commissioned. Land belonging to Oxford and Cambridge colleges was also mapped, with these surviving in the appropriate college libraries. Most, though, are held in county record offices, some at the National Archives and the British Library, and number in their tens of thousands in total. Their existence and survival is patchy, as it is with all pre-OS maps. For Kent, a little over a quarter of its parishes are covered (before the eighteenth century) by estate maps, for example.

Very few medieval estate maps exist, for surveying was then a written not a graphic exercise. In the later sixteenth century, surveying methods had improved considerably, so estate maps began to be made in quantity. The redistribution of land during the reformation and Commonwealth resulted in land surveys being made. The greatest age for estate maps was the eighteenth and early nineteenth centuries, however, as standards were high. However, with the coming of the OS, maps began to be based on these accurate maps and the golden age of the estate map was over.

Another major collection of plans is that held at the Victoria and Albert Museum in London, of the Royal Institute of British Architects' drawings. These are mostly of prominent buildings, large country or town houses, public buildings and churches, though there are some of smaller premises, too. There are indexes.

Borough Guides, published throughout the twentieth centuries, often included a map of the locality in question. They will be of towns or suburbs but not villages. These usually include named streets, parks and prominent buildings such as churches and schools. They do not show individual buildings and detail is usually lacking. Yet for an overall view of a town, they are useful because they show it at a single glance, whereas usually several OS maps are needed to view any but the smallest of settlements. Maps also often featured in directories from the eighteenth to the twentieth centuries.

Maps and plans also feature in deeds to property, which, in the later nineteenth and twentieth centuries, tend to include a block plan of the property sold or rented. These will show the extent of the garden/yard, location of other adjoining properties as well as nearby streets. They are often colour coded for ease.

A more recent, but geographically limited series of maps are the Goad plans, made for insurance purposes from the 1960s and updated

Guildhall Library. (Author)

annually. They do not show residential properties but focus on principal commercial districts, chiefly high streets, labelling the shops by name. They are very useful for showing changes over time. With a scale of 40 inches to the mile they are more detailed than the OS maps. Large collections can be seen at the British Library, London Metropolitan Archives and the Guildhall Library, but those for a particular district should be found in the appropriate local studies library.

Maps can be found in local record offices and libraries for the particular district that the institution covers. The largest collections can be found in a number of national repositories. Principal among these are at the British Library in their Map Room, which includes all the OS maps of the country, and at the National Archives (under WO44, 47 and 55). The Bodleian Library also has a substantial cartographic collection, including the first known map of Great Britain to show roads, the

Gough Map of 1375. The Library's map collection includes 1.25 million maps and 20,000 atlases (not just of Britain); 113 of the latter are maps of England from 1677 to 1835. Many of the older maps can be viewed online, of course.

Many record offices and record societies have published listings of maps in their collections, with commentaries on the maps and their makers. These are often illustrated with scaled-down illustrations of the maps in question. This can be a valuable method of ascertaining what exists before a visit to the record office is made – as well as checking their online catalogue, of course.

Maps are very useful for showing the built, or rural, environs, that your ancestors lived in. Even if you visit the place where they lived (which is recommended and discussed in Chapter 8), it is almost certain that the place will have altered to a lesser or larger extent. These maps will show what it was like at the time that they lived there. If your ancestors lived in the same village or town for a considerable period, the study of several editions of maps of the same district will show how it changed over time; perhaps revealing how a place became industrialised or/and how new roads and houses were built, and as garages were constructed and other forms of transport came to a district, such as railways or canals.

Chapter 5

NEWSPAPERS

'The Press, Watson, is a most valuable institution, if you only know how to use it', as Sherlock Holmes commented to his friend in *The Adventure of the Six Napoleons*. There is such a great quantity of national and local newspapers in libraries and local studies centres that this sheer volume can appear forbidding. For an overview of newspapers, see www.cyndislist.com/newspapers.

There has been a newspaper industry, of sorts, in Britain since 1622, but the early titles were short-lived; the first to have a long life was *The London Gazette*, which began as *The Oxford Gazette*, in 1665, before being renamed in the following year. Initially it appeared twice weekly and then daily. It gave official announcements, but relatively little news as such. In 1702 *The Daily Courant* became Britain's first daily (excepting Sundays) and was a single sheet of paper, double-sided. Most newspapers were published in London, but had a wide circulation elsewhere. The regional press developed in the eighteenth century, based in the major towns and cities, such as *The Newcastle Courant* in 1712 and *The Northampton Mercury* of 1720. Some cities had more than one newspaper.

One reason for the relatively limited array of eighteenth-century newspapers was that they were taxed. A stamp duty was imposed on newspapers in 1712. The tax was initially one penny for a folded sheet, but increased and had risen to four pence in 1815. The duty was reduced to a penny in 1836 and was finally abolished altogether in 1861. This resulted in a flood of new publications which could charge less now the tax was no longer due. This growth was also because of increases in both population and literacy. Newspapers probably were most informative towards the end of the nineteenth and the beginning of the twentieth century.

The content of newspapers has varied considerably over the centuries. Eighteenth-century newspapers contained a great deal of overseas news, mostly from Europe, much national news and a little local news, known as Country News. Indeed, local newspapers had little local news. Military, political and diplomatic news could take up much space. So did news of crimes and the verdicts of the Assize courts were usually featured when they took place. Births, deaths and marriages of the socially prominent would be reported, as would unusual events and strange deaths. Sport and fashion were rarely reported. Advertisements were a prominent feature, however, and could take up to half the space. These included adverts for property and other goods for sale and references to bankruptcies. Adverts can shed a light on local society. They can show farms for sale or for let, and sales of livestock and agricultural equipment. Shops selling farm essentials often listed their wares with prices. Markets were announced, with details of time, location, produce and other details.

There was also news of ships arriving at British ports and share prices. Letters from other parts of the country reporting on newsworthy events were a regular feature. Newspapers often pasted verbatim articles from other newspapers. They were rarely illustrated and their print-runs were usually modest.

Nineteenth-century newspapers tended to be longer. They also were usually far more detailed in their reporting of debates in Parliament and trials of serious crimes, for instance. As the century progressed they included other features. These were letters from readers, fiction, often in serial format, and an editorial on major events of the day. As sport began to be more organised, matches were reported, especially cricket and football, in the appropriate seasons. The doings of clubs and societies, churches and schools were other staples, as well as announcements for entertainments. Obituaries of individuals began to be printed, rather than just a line or two announcing a death as before. Personal columns listing births, marriages and deaths, paid for by the inserter, made their appearance. Local newspapers still often included national and international stories, presumably in the belief that readers would only buy one newspaper. Front pages would often be dominated by adverts (*The Times* maintained this custom until 1965). Again, illustrations were unusual. *The Illustrated Police News* broke new ground by its line drawings and lurid headlines from 1864. National newspapers now tended to be daily and appeared on Sundays, too. Local newspapers were invariably weekly, appearing on Fridays or Saturdays, but some were daily or twice weekly.

Adverts on front page of the Middlesex County Times, *1876. (London Borough of Ealing)*

The twentieth century, with universal literacy now prevalent, saw a new breed of newspapers being created. There were new titles and old titles adapted, merged, changed their name or folded. They included more and more illustrations and some had prominent headlines. Features aimed at children and women began to appear. Print was larger and pages greater in number. National news and international news began to be banished from the local press, though letters pages often reflected controversies based on these events, as well as more local concerns. Towards the end of the twentieth century, some newspapers were made available free of charge and many appeared online. Local newspapers found themselves squeezed by rival news providers, though ever since the widespread availability of wireless and television news this had been an issue. Although there have been falls in circulation, the newspaper industry is still alive, but the local press is largely less informative and detailed in the early twenty-first century than it was a century ago.

Cities and towns have newspapers with their own name in its title; for example *The York Courant* in the eighteenth or *The Keighley News* in the following century. Small towns and villages may well not have a newspaper explicitly devoted to their own affairs, because of their small size; often a county may have one or more newspapers devoted to county affairs, such as the nineteenth-century titles, *The Buckinghamshire Advertiser* and *The Middlesex County Times*. Yet these newspapers often have a page or two which cover the towns and villages in that county and have a paragraph titled with that place's news.

Newspapers were not all the same. Many had clear political standpoints, reflected both in editorials and in the letters pages. They can put across arguments for political reform at national or at local level, or bring to the readers' attention perceived local abuses and issues, such as high rates, a polluted river or the cost of a new town hall. Local newspapers tended to have a bias, though not necessarily party political. This was especially the case if there was more than one newspaper for a particular district. Nationals also varied in their content, with some aiming at a low-brow readership and others at a more intelligent and educated clientele.

As with photographs and maps, newspapers for a particular district are usually to be found in the library or local studies centre covering that district. There are also two major national centres of newspaper holdings. One is the Bodleian Library at Oxford, with a collection of seventeenth- and eighteenth-century newspapers. The other is the British Library. There are two main collections here. One is in the Rare Books Room, and this is the Burney Collection of eighteenth-century newspapers on microfilm which can be very easily accessed by consulting the catalogues on the shelves and then going to the self-service microfilms which are very nearby.

The more substantial collection is the one which was held at the British Library Newspaper Library at Colindale in north London until 2013. It has now been moved to the main British Library site on the Euston Road, which makes life much easier as the trek from central London on the Northern Line can now be avoided. The collection includes most national and local newspapers published in Britain, and some overseas titles, since the seventeenth century. It is far from complete, however, with some newspapers being held elsewhere and some simply not having survived. Some of the major national and Sunday newspapers of the nineteenth and twentieth centuries are on open access, which is a great help. The vast majority, though, need to be ordered; some can take 70 minutes to arrive providing the order is made before 4pm; others may need longer (at least two days for paper copies), but orders can be made online prior to visiting. Some are viewed on microfilm and others in hard copy.

For those who are not able to visit London, electronic access to newspapers, usually for a fee, is an attractive option. Initially only a handful of national newspapers were available in this format, such as *The Times* (1785–1985) and the *Daily Mirror* from 1905. More recently, the British Library has been digitalising newspapers in the collection, and though only a small proportion have been digitalised, this is still a considerable number: see www.britishnewspaperarchive.co.uk. In both cases, the entire text can be searched by any search term desired and can be refined by dates. Any reference to the term in the press can be found; a name in an advert, in a letter, in a court case, anything. Access is through a subscription site (per month). Some institutions, such as the British Library, subscribe to such sites and so a researcher can view them there free of charge.

Apart from these, there are often card indexes or paper indexes to local newspapers held by local studies centres. These are very useful, but are inevitably limited compared to the electronic versions referred to above. Even the best indexes cannot include every single item that might be of conceivable interest to researchers. For example, every instance of petty crime or every property advert could not be included in such indexes.

The uses of local newspapers to the family historian are, perhaps, to an extent, obvious. There are obituaries, announcements of births, marriages and deaths. Prominent individuals and families, such as the nobility, clergy, gentry, local politicians, those in business, or particularly notorious ones (which could include those already mentioned) will also have their doings reported. Most people, though, rarely figure in newspapers.

But if your ancestors were, like most people, rarely if ever newsworthy, this does not mean that newspapers are of no interest to the family historian. Looking through a selection of newspapers for the town for the period that your ancestor lived in it, or at least a selection of them, gives an insight into their lives that no other source can give. Of course the information given in newspapers is often biased and certainly incomplete, though the latter can be said about any historical source. But they do offer an immediacy that no other source can offer, because they reflect facts and views of the time, unfiltered and unselected by historians.

These are the newspapers that your ancestors would have read, or perhaps, in the early nineteenth or eighteenth century, have had read to them (this often occurred in pubs). They may also have taken part in some of the activities described or have witnessed them. They therefore allow the family historian an insight into their lives, which helps them become more than names in census returns or electoral registers.

CASE STUDIES
Taken from The Buckinghamshire Advertiser, 1870.

HILLINGDON
PLEASURE FAIR- This event came off with the highest resplendency that naptha can convey last Saturday, and was the largest congregation of peculiarities that has been seen in the locality for many years. The weather was extremely warm, and the visitors very

numerous, and all sorts of succulent and suspicious trifles of food and remarkable drinks were bought up with avidity from garish looking damsels and gipsy looking men. The compressibility of the human frame was studied in all the tavern entrances. Several distinguished caterers were present, one of whom gained renown by inducing small birds to execute very indifferent, though unnatural, exploits, another by exhibiting a prodigiously corpulent female, who had become expanded by some extraordinary physical process, whilst under a natural bower of elm trees several fair creatures could be seen displaying their sylphide forms on a platform of a circus tent, entrancing the rustic gaze with their serial gyrations. These were, in short, a variety of shows containing different wonders, but as it is reported that an adventure into the interior of such places is almost as 'risky' as sleeping with a Russian, we waived exploring their contents, an example, which we are proud to say, on the behalf of the proprietors, was not followed by humanity in general, who flocked into their depths both numerously and tumultuously. Extra police were in attendance, and all went off without mishap.

UXBRIDGE GAS

For some time past the inhabitants of Uxbridge have been endeavouring, but until recently without success, to discover the cause of certain noxious smells that have been prevalent in the streets, in our shops, and private houses. Now, however, there is no doubt that the various surmises indulged in were incorrect, and that to the impurity of the gas supplied by the Uxbridge and Hillingdon Gas Company may be traced the sole cause of the abominable stenches which have met us at every turn. To be satisfied upon the point, we have applied the simple sugar-of-lead-test and have found sulphuretted hydrogen present in the gas in large quantities. This is a state of things that should not, and must not exist; for surely if our tradesmen are content to pay a long price for the use of the article, they have a right, at least, to expect that they shall not be inconvenienced by being compelled to put out their lights, as we understand has been the case, at the time they most need them. The remedy is very simple. In proof of this latter statement we extract a few observations from an authority on the subject: 'The gas and its accompanying vapours are next made to traverse a refrigerator, usually a series of iron pipes, cooled on the outside by a stream of water; there the condensation of the tar and ammonical liquid becomes complete, and the gas proceeds onwards to another part of the apparatus, in which it is to be deprived of the sulphuretted hydrogen and carbonic acid gasses always present in the crude product'. The neglect of the latter portion of the process would appear, therefore, to be the cause of the complaint the public can raise against the gas authorities, whose duty it imperatively is to at once adopt proper remedies, or, in other words, to give us pure gas with as little delay as possible.

Now, if you had an ancestor who lived in Hillingdon or Uxbridge in 1870 it is highly likely that they would have gone to the first event and have experienced the less amusing second. We cannot know what their opinion of the fair was. Clearly the journalist was not impressed, and made the proverbial 'swift exit' of journalists at moments of potential risk and embarrassment. Most people seem to have enjoyed it and relished a day on which they could partake of exotic entertainment to spice up what may well have been a pretty humdrum, routine rural existence. These extracts certainly help create a picture of events in the past which no other source can.

Editorials provide useful commentary on the state of local affairs in a given week. Take *The Southall News* in the winter of 1886:

It unfortunately happened, too that during the fortnight after the Christmas week, ie, during the school holidays, the penny dinner institution so nobly founded by W.F. Thomas, Esq., of Manor House, Southall Green was closed, so that the luxury of a hot mid-day meal for the children was not available to help out the meagre provision poor parents were able to afford for their families during the severe weather of the latter half of last week. That the penny dinner is appreciated as a boon may be inferred from the fact that as early as Friday last upwards of 500 dinner tickets had been purchased in anticipation of the re-opening of the institution, announced for Monday the 11th instant. That there are a few whom the dinners are intended to benefit who are not grateful is a matter of course, for such, too, 'are always with us'.

The chief difficulty in the way of obtaining the dinners to lie in the fact that the poor have not the pennies wherewith to purchase them, and with the earth sealed against the spade, and all other out of labour rendered well-nigh impossible by the frost, their condition is saddening to contemplate, and while the frost lasts will daily become worse.

Sport is a common feature of the press, with usually a page or two's coverage in each issue. While football or cricket, depending on the season tend to dominate, other sports are also reported, as noted in a July copy of *The West Middlesex Gazette* of 1930:

CYCLING
EALING CLUB'S RUN
Aylesbury, the venue of Sunday's run by members of the Ealing Cycling Club, was reached in good time for lunch, after a halt at Amersham. A short run brought the club to Tring, where after a walk through Lord Rothschild's Park and a visit to the Nell Gwynne monument, tea was served. The homeward run led through Chesham to picturesque Chorley Wood and Rickmansworth.

Tomorrow, after the open 50 miles T.T. for the John Bull Tyre Trophy, tea will be served at Oldfield's, Maidenhead.

MOTOR CYCLING
MIDNIGHT SOCIAL RUN
There will be an all-night social run to-night (Saturday) by members of the West Ealing Motor and Motor Cycle Club, starting from the Ace of Spades Garage, Great West Road at 12 midnight. The first stop will be at the Devil's Punch Bowl, Hindhead for coffee, then onto Houghton, Sussex, for breakfast. Members will then make for Goring-on-Sea to complete the day.

On the subject of printed matter, sermons were a popular type of publication in the eighteenth and nineteenth centuries, as difficult as that may be to fathom now. A great many clergymen, not all of whom were well known, had sermons published, advertised in *The Gentleman's Magazine* and elsewhere and being sold for sixpence. These might well be focusing on a particular political or religious event, whether national or local.

Given churchgoing was at a high rate in these centuries, your ancestor may well have been on the receiving end of these sermons, so to speak. Sermons were often bought by the literate and read out to their families. Many published sermons can be found at the British Library. You can search by typing 'sermon' and the village/town where your ancestor resided into the online British Library catalogue, and ascertaining whether these were published at the time of your ancestor. Of course, for each clergyman, only a few sermons were published and fewer survive. Furthermore, those that do may well not be representative of a parson's output.

Ideally, one should read the newspaper for the town or village at the time when your ancestors lived there. That will give an impression of public events in that locality. Your ancestor may not, and probably will not, be mentioned by name. But it is likely that they may have participated in the events described and would certainly have been aware of them. They may or may not have read the same newspaper, depending on their literacy level, but newspapers were often read aloud in public places in the eighteenth century, for instance. This is a time-consuming process and so sampling may have to be resorted to, though this runs the danger of missing information that one would otherwise have gained.

However, the process need not be as lengthy as reading through whole newspapers. Since local newspapers in the eighteenth and nineteenth centuries (and often beyond) covered national and international news, these stories can be ignored. Furthermore, newspapers often had specific headings for villages and towns in their remit and so all the news about a particular place would be under one heading and clearly marked with the name of that town/village. Newspapers tend to be organised in the same fashion from issue to issue, so if the national news is on page 2 then that can be passed over without delay, and if the news on particular places is on page 3, then only one page per issue needs to be scanned, and within that only one column. Editorials can often be omitted, if they are a commentary on national or overseas news, such as a war, but editorial comment often concerns local issues, too. Editorials often reveal the newspaper's political and religious prejudices in a more obvious way than reporting of events, and so are helpful for a reader concerned with bias in the newspaper more general. Whether adverts, which often appeared on the front page, should be ignored is another question; probably not if

Gentleman's Magazine, *title-page (London Borough of Ealing)*

your ancestors were in trade, because their competitors may well have advertised (as they may well have done themselves). And, of course, your ancestors may well have responded to the adverts by purchasing the goods and services in question.

There are also specialist publications which may be useful. First, there was the *Political State of Great Britain* from 1711–40 and *The Gentleman's Magazine* of 1731–1868 (these latter can be seen, along with some other newspapers at www.bodley.ox.ac.uk/ilej but these full text copies are not searchable by keyword). They were arranged month by month and, as with eighteenth-century newspapers, covered national, local and international news in The Historical Chronicle. A couple of examples from this Chronicle from *The Gentleman's Magazine* of November 1762 are as follows:

Wednesday 27 October
Early in the morning, the inhabitants of Norwich were surprised with a sudden inundation, which overflowed all the lower parts of the city, and laid under water between 2 and 3000 houses, and 8 parish churches. The flood continued all Wednesday, but abated on Thursday morning. It was 13 inches higher than the flood called St. Faith's Flood in 1696, not so high as the great flood in 1646, by 8 inches; nor as St. Andrew's flood in 1614, by 13 inches. In many of the streets, boats were plying to carry provisions, and assist the distressed. The water is thought to have risen about 12 feet perpendicular. The loss to the inhabitants is supposed to be near 10,000l.

Many people, in other places, suffered irreparably by the swelling of the waters on this memorable occasion, an imperfect account of which has already been given. It were to be wished, however, that our correspondents would transmit from the several places where the floods rose remarkably, an authentic account of the damages done in their respective neighbourhoods, the accounts hitherto published in the papers, being ether much exaggerated, or very defective.

Wednesday 3 November
A man about 60 years of age, stood on the pillory in Cheapside for a detestable crime. The populace fell upon the wretch, tore off

his coat, waistcoat, shirt, hat, wig & breeches, and then pelted and whipped him till he had scarcely any signs of life left; but he was once pulled off the pillory, but hung by his arms till he was set up again, and stood in that naked condition, covered with mud, till the hour was out, and then he was carried back to Newgate.

They covered national news and the arts, economic and financial news, but also included genealogical information and topographical material. Some of the latter was republished separately by county in 1892, in a number of volumes, arranged alphabetically by county and then by parish. This included recording from monumental inscriptions and parish registers and descriptions of ancient and medieval remains. Prints and maps of buildings, towns and counties often appeared therein. These can be found on the open shelves of the British Library Rare Books room and the National Archives.

The built environment of the nineteenth and twentieth centuries can be studied via a number of contemporary journals. *The Builder* was established in 1843 and was a weekly magazine devoted to architecture and construction. Many public and private buildings feature, and each year it had an index to properties. It merges with *The Building News* (established in 1855), which had a similar remit. *Country Life* is well known for its articles and adverts for country houses, of varying sizes, but from its inception in 1897 has included articles about country districts which may be of interest. The works of civil engineers from sewers to bridges can be found online in *The Engineer* (from 1856) on www.gracesguide.co.uk. Despite its name, *The Illustrated London News*, initially weekly from 1842 but later monthly, featured articles about events elsewhere in the country and was always profusely illustrated (unlike many newspapers of the nineteenth century).

What newspapers often cannot do, though, is to describe everyday life. They are there to report news; events which are deemed out of the ordinary run of life's events. So, for a village, reports of the population working on the land is unlikely to be reported except if there is some sort of celebration to mark the harvest being brought in, or if there is an accident to persons or property. The latter can often shed light on the ordinary processes, if, for example, an inquest had to be held on a farm labourer who was killed by machinery, say.

There is also a need for caution in accepting everything a newspaper reports as being accurate. First, newspaper reports about an event that happened in the past (at time of writing) should never be accepted at face value without checking sources written at the time of the said event. Second, reporting may not be comprehensive, so it is impossible to know what has been omitted. For example, letters from evacuated children reproduced in the press in the Second World War rarely contain any complaints, because a positive spin was required.

Newspapers as a source for events cannot be ignored by the local and family historian. How much time one spends with them is another question and that can only be decided by the researcher and the quality of the reporting. However, most people find reading old newspapers surprisingly addictive once begun and it is easy to become distracted from one's main line of enquiry. It is common for stories and letters to continue over a number of issues and these can resemble chapters of a story that can make quite compelling reading.

Chapter 6

LOCAL ARCHIVES

The obvious source for local history are local history libraries (which hold archives), borough or county record offices, established from the 1920s to the 1970s. Most readers will be familiar with these, for their holdings of information in a narrow number of sources which relate directly to their ancestors, for example, parish registers, local census returns, militia lists and so on. Local archives are under the jurisdiction of a local government unit, usually a county or a borough council, and are usually financed and administered by them. They are not the only source of relevant archives, as we will learn in the next chapter, but they are important and probably should be the first port of call. This is not just for the information they contain, but also because of the staff there. They will know the collections well from having worked there for some time, possibly many years, and may well have lectured on aspects of their district's local history or even have written local history books.

Local Government
The archives in these places have accrued over many years. Their core is the records of the administration of the jurisdiction and its predecessor bodies and often date back some centuries (in the case of ancient boroughs, to the early Middle Ages). It should be noted that archives are defined by being the records created by an individual or body of people in the course of their existence; they were not created for the future use of researchers but for an immediate business need. Once their original use has passed, a decision has been taken that they be preserved for research purposes. Most records do not survive (school admission registers are a common casualty), their creators or their successors having decided to dispose of them once they have ceased to be immediately useful – though if they had done otherwise there would not be the space, the money or the staff to care for them. What does survive often does so because of luck.

Archives were often kept in the Town Clerk's department, but as the twentieth century progressed, councils financed record office departments to house, conserve, list and make available these records for public consultation. Legislation in the 1950s and 1960s allowed local government to spend money on the preservation of their records. As time passed, these places collected other archives, those of people and organisations within the same jurisdiction as its parent body, as defined by their collection policies. By the 1970s all English counties had a record office, sometimes in one location, sometimes in more than one. Many were located in the headquarters building of the local authority, but increasingly due to the demands of additional space, for record collections are not static and records accrue over time, they were housed in purpose-built record offices.

So what records can a researcher expect to find here? Often researchers concentrate solely on a narrow range of sources, such as

London Borough of Hillingdon Local History Centre. (Author)

parish registers or other documents which list individuals, but these are only the tip of the iceberg. The parish was not just a religious body, but the basic unit of local government in England from the seventeenth to the nineteenth centuries. They dealt with the care of the poor (under the terms of the Old Poor Law of 1601–1834), the upkeep of law and order, saw to repairs of bridges, roads and the church within the parish. It was not just a case of baptisms, marriages and burials. In the course of their business they created records as they wrote down the decisions taken at meetings.

The governing body of the parish was the vestry, a group of parishioners including the vicar, who made decisions about raising and spending money and selected men to carry out their resolutions. These executive officers were the churchwardens (who cared for the church fabric), the overseer/s (who oversaw the poor law) and the constable/s. There might also be a surveyor of the highway who dealt with the roads and bridges. All these kept accounts of their expenditure in order to be reimbursed at the end of their annual term of office. Some of these accounts are simple totals of money; others are itemised, listing exactly how much was spent and on what or on whom. These are far the more valuable because they show what the officers did.

Vestry minutes record the decisions taken by the vestry members, after noting the date of the meeting and those men who attended it. Those for the meeting after Easter include setting the rate to be levied on the parish's ratepayers and choosing the officials for the year, as well as settling the accounts of the outgoing officials. Other meetings will discuss matters of policy.

The following illustration is from the Parish of Hanwell's Vestry Minute Books:

Friday December 27 1805
At a Vestry holden this day
Present
The Revd. Mr Glasse – Rector
Mr Fownes – Churchwardens
Mr Green
Mr Bramsgrove – Overseer
Mr Compson
Mr Williams Mr Jakell

Mr Chamberlain

Mr Bailey

John Whitmore applied for charity – agreed that he is a proper object for the establishment at Islington under the care of Mr Mackenzie. Agreed to allow him the sume lined, and three shillings a week during the month of January at the end of which time (if he is chargeable) agreed to send him of Mr Mackenzie's.

Thomas Ball appeared, and stated, that he was afflicted with rheumatism and totally unable to maintain his family – that his cart and horse had been seized – that his business was at an end – and his rent beyond his ability to pay.

Agreed to put him into one of the vacant houses in the half acre – and to allow him 7s a week for the support of his family – viz. Wm. Aged 13, a cripple – James aged eleven years – Henry aged nine years, and George aged seven years.

Agreed to send the boy William to the hospital, if approved by Mr Morris.

George Henry Glasse

Jno. Fownes

Thos. Green

Thos. Bramsgrove.

Apart from mentioning individuals – vestry members and those assisted – it also shows the working of the poor law in the said parish, which effects would have been known to fellow parishioners. If you can find such records for a parish at the time when your ancestor lived there, then this provides a background to their lives.

The other key body in local government at this time were the justices of the peace in the quarter sessions in the counties, and corporations headed by a mayor and aldermen in larger towns and cities. The quarter sessions was made up of justices of the peace, usually county gentlemen and clergy, who met formally in session four times a year. These were chiefly responsible for law and order, but they also dealt with the lower tier of local government, the parishes, arbitrating between them when they fell into dispute (usually over whose responsibility it was to pay poor relief to particular parties). Corporations also served to regulate trade and often provided basic infrastructure.

Both these types of organisation created records. Their core records were the minute or order books; they recorded similar types of information as the vestry minutes, but also on occasions of great pageantry and national importance.

The Oxford Corporation noted on 12 March 1702:

A proclamation of the accession of Princess Anne of Denmark as Queen of England having been received and the mayor acquainting the house that he intends the celebration to take place this day, it is agreed that for the honour of this 'Solemnity' a quantity of claret be spent by putting it into the conduit and running it in two pipes, eastwards and southwards, and that so many barrels of beer be spent among the freemen and such other entertainments for the Council Chamber be provided as thought fit and all expenses shall be borne by the City. For the order and solemnity it is agreed that it be on horseback: the Mayor and Recorder to ride with foot cloths, the Mayor, aldermen, thirteen bailiffs, and such others who have had been bailiffs and have gowns, to ride in their scarlet gowns, and such other members of the house who have good horses to ride in their gowns and take horse at the Guildhall; then John Moulden to ride first to make way; next the petty constables on foot with their long staves; then the trumpeters, the bailiffs' serjeants with their maces; then the bailiffs with their white staves; then the town clerk and the macebearer with the great mace; then the Mayor, the Recorder, and the senior aldermen, then the rest of the thirteen, two and two; and all such as have been bailiffs and have scarlet gowns to ride in seniority next the thirteen, and then such members as have good horses to ride next in seniority.

The order of proclamation to be done in the places and manner following:- the proclamation is to be first made at Carfax, on the east side of the conduit, to ride thence to St. Mary's and there do it again, thence to East Gate and then back again over to Carfax and to the South Gate, starting at the 'Laine's End' and there do it again, thence through Pennyfarthing Street to West Gate and then do it again, and thence up the old Butcher Row and so over Carfax again to the North Gate and then proclaim it again and from thence back again over Carfax to the Guildhall again.

This, then, relates what happened when Oxford celebrated the accession of the new monarch, Queen Anne, when she succeeded to the throne in 1702. It is probably safe to assume that most residents would have attended, even if only to add a little colour to their otherwise humdrum lives, rather than to show their allegiance to the new monarch. It was clearly a colourful spectacle, and with drink flowing free of charge, an enjoyable one. It is probable that, if your ancestors resided in the city or were at one of the colleges at this time, they would have known about these celebrations and probably attended as spectators and had some of the free drink.

In the nineteenth century, central government demanded more and more of local government, to meet the perceived changing needs of the country, especially in the fields of public health, poverty and infrastructure. Parishes united with their neighbours to undertake some tasks, notably poor relief, following the introduction of the New Poor Law of 1834, leading to Boards of Guardians being formed to build workhouses, in which poor relief was increasingly, though by no means universally, administered (for useful background material, see www.workhouses.org.uk). Lighting and drainage and the provision of cemeteries were three major issues resulting from legislation aimed at improving the health of the country. Initially no new forms of government were introduced, but vestries established subcommittees to deal with the work required and by reading their minutes we can see how a community was changing. Additional bodies came into being to regulate lighting and burials. New legislation led to Local Boards of Health being created, with additional powers as those of the parishes were diminished. All these bodies created records of their decisions and actions.

In 1888 the Local Government Act led to the creation of county councils, and from 1894, urban and rural district councils; quarter sessions were reduced to being criminal courts, as their administrative role was passed to the county councils. These new bodies were made up of elected representatives and they employed professional and permanent salaried employees (the parishes did not, on the whole, pay salaries). They were also given the responsibility for many public duties. They governed by committees, each with differing responsibilities. Likewise, in the towns, corporations became increasingly bureaucratic and professional. Throughout the twentieth century, councils took on more and more powers, such as over health, housing and education. Beneath the rural and urban district councils were parish councils (not to be confused, as in *The Vicar of Dibley*, with the parochial church councils, which dealt with purely religious matters), whose powers were very local and limited, and they are also creators of records to provide evidence of their activity.

The system has remained roughly the same since then, but there have been changes. Some boroughs have merged to form fewer but larger units. In 1974 the county system changed; the West Riding of Yorkshire split between the newly created West Yorkshire and South Yorkshire; the East Riding became part of the newly created Humberside; in the southwest a new county termed Avon was created, and Cumberland and Westmorland became Cumbria. Rutland was absorbed into Lincolnshire. In the 1990s, some of these county boundaries were altered yet again.

All these councils have generated an immense amount of paper, recording what they did, just as the county and quarter sessions had. Many of these public records date back centuries; those of corporations may date back to the Middle Ages; those of the parish to the sixteenth century. Yet unbroken runs of centuries of records cannot be taken for granted. Minute books usually survive, but additional papers – drafts, plans, accounts –may not always do so.

We should also reconsider traditional family history sources. Parish registers are a well-known source for family historians to track down baptisms, marriages and burials of family members. Once this has been done, they are unlikely to be reused. Yet they do have a further value. Parish registers are also a key source for the local historian, especially one interested in population history prior to the national census of 1801. They tell a great deal about aspects of a community's history. For instance, if in one particular year there are but ten baptisms and your ancestor's is amongst them, it suggests that the birth of a child was relatively unusual and therefore more significant than it would have been in a well-populated parish. Or if there were a large number of deaths in a plague year and your ancestors were not among them, this suggests they may have left the district temporarily or were very lucky indeed. In any case, the plague made an impact on their lives. Or were there many deaths at the same time as one of your ancestors died? If so, this puts their deaths into their local context. Clergymen often made comments about local people and events in the margins of these registers, which can give additional insights into contemporary life.

The same reasoning can be applied to poor law records which often feature significantly within parish archives as the parish dealt with the poor law from 1601 to 1834 and often beyond. If an ancestor is found to have been in receipt of poor relief, check the records to see who else received it. Were the amounts (or goods) received different? Were the payments made for different periods of time? If many men were in receipt of such benefits it suggests a local or national economic depression leading to unemployment. Or for an elderly person, it may be interesting to note how many others were in receipt of pension payments. Once an ancestor's name has been found in parish records, look at the adjacent pages of the same source, which will tell more about the parish they lived in and ultimately more about their own lives.

The Boards of Guardians dealt with poor relief following the introduction of the New Poor Law in 1834. These were bodies made up of representatives from a number of parishes, often adjacent to one another and known as Unions. They often built workhouses in order to house the poor who were in need of relief, but they did not wholly obliterate the older tradition of outdoor relief. These bodies created records of their activities, in building the workhouses and administering them. Admission and discharge registers, creed registers and indoor relief registers are the usual sources sought after by family historians as the other sources (e.g. minutes of the Guardians' meetings, annual reports and accounts) do not list names of inmates. Yet the minute books give an insight into conditions at the workhouse. Plans show what the workhouse looked like (especially valuable because often the original buildings are long demolished or if not are used for a wholly different purpose).

In the later nineteenth century, decisions were taken not only by the full council, but by numerous committees, made up of councillors, officials and specially picked members of the public with relevant knowledge and experience. They dealt with a great number of issues including finance, public health, public housing (these two were especially important after 1918), works (which included granting permission for construction – or not – to builders and for the erection of infrastructure such as street lighting), public libraries, parks and open spaces and many others. During the World Wars there were additional committees for the duration of the conflicts, dealing with civil defence, recruitment and so forth. Minute books note the decisions taken at these monthly or weekly meetings, of policies, proposals, action to be taken, by whom and when, expenditure to be undertaken and the progress of action already ordered.

The number of these minute books makes their examination seem daunting, especially if the indexes are non-existent or rudimentary at best. Yet not all will be relevant; finance is unlikely to be so; likewise parks and libraries. Yet the Housing Committee minutes may be of use if your ancestors lived in the council housing which could be built from the mid-nineteenth century but which was rarely built until after 1918, and more so, after 1945. These minute books could well provide background information on the houses or flats that your ancestors inhabited. Civil defence minute books could also be useful for life in a locality during the World Wars, and are more likely to be franker than accounts in the censored local press of the time.

Civil defence archives were created during the Second World War as the responsibilities of local authorities were expanded to deal with the emergency created by war. They do not always survive, but where they do they can be very extensive. They can deal with information about air raid incidents, listing where bombs fell, what damage they did, type of bomb and details of the recovery operation. Property was requisitioned either to be used as emergency accommodation for families whose homes were destroyed in bombing, or to be used as furniture stores for damaged properties. Open land, including parks and commons, was set aside for allotments in order to help grow more food. Papers dealing with this often include plans and regulations and even names of allotment holders. Listings of public air raid shelters and correspondence about their construction and decommissioning can be found among these files. Air raid warning posts and equipment issued to workers can also be detailed in these files. As these papers were not generally public, they can include criticisms and difficulties faced on the Home Front that would not have been publicised at the time.

Both World Wars resulted in war memorials being made to commemorate the sacrifices made by the locality's population. These can vary considerably. Not everywhere has a war memorial as such, but there was usually a committee formed to debate what should be done. Often, as well as a memorial with names, there might be more practical ways to assist the families of the fallen, such as putting aside money raised for scholarships or other educational uses for children who had lost their father.

Local authorities were also responsible for schooling from the late nineteenth century and so education archives often survive within their holdings. Often the family historian can restrict themselves to admission registers and less often punishment books. However, these records, especially the former, rarely survive, mostly because their use is apparently over when the particular intake of pupils a book covers no longer attends the school. They are only required to be kept for three years after their final date in any case and may be closed for lengthy periods due to data protection legislation.

Overlooked, though they survive in far greater quantities, are school log books. Often neglected because they very rarely mention pupils by name unless for exceptional reasons, they are an invaluable source for the history of a particular school. If you can learn which school your ancestor/s attended, perhaps through the admission registers (which give little information save the name of the pupil, their address, father's name, date of birth and years at the school), then the log books are worth inspecting. The headteacher was obliged by law to keep a record of activity at the school, in chronological order.

The 'Instructions by the Board of Education on keeping of a School Log Book' read as follows:

> It must be kept by the principal teacher, who is required to enter in it, from time to time, such events as the introduction of new books, apparatus or course of instruction, any plan of lessons approved by the Board, the visits of managers, absence, illness, or failure of duty, on the part of any of the school staff, or as any special circumstances affecting the school, that may, for the sake of future reference, or for any other reason, deserve to be recorded. No reflections or opinions of a general character are to be entered in the log book.

The events noted also include school inspections, with results, examinations, visits by civic and religious dignitaries, health workers and occasionally celebrities. Class visits outside the school and sports days will be noted, as well as the beginning and end of terms. Special days such as those marking the end of World Wars, or Empire Day, will be noted, as are evacuation and air raids during wartime. If many pupils are absent due to a local outbreak of illness or the needs of harvesting or bad weather, these too will be recorded. Absences of teachers and their replacement by supply teachers are included. What are not included are everyday routine events, such as lessons.

Less common are minute books of the school's governing body; meetings of school governors or managers, or of the councillors who determined school policy and major projects. These will be even less likely to mention individual pupils, but they should deal with higher level matters which will have had an impact on a particular school/s and issues that were causing concern at particular schools. Appointment of headteachers and infrastructure is also covered in these books.

Businesses and Clubs
Local archives hold far more than the records of their parent body. Their remit, as established by their collection policy, is usually defined geographically by that of their parent body. They, therefore, collect archives of other organisations within that remit. These can include religious and political organisations, charities, clubs and societies and companies which either existed in the past and no longer do so, or perhaps still exist, and have decided to let the archives have some or all of their records in order to save them space and allow them to be used by members of the public for research purposes.

These records can include the club's constitution/rules, minute books, treasurer's papers and account books, annual reports/AGM agendas and minutes, membership lists, papers relating to the events that an organisation promoted. For a sports club these might include annual fixture lists of matches and social events. There might be correspondence files with possible and actual sponsors. Magazines and pamphlets produced might also feature therein. There may be photographs and memorabilia. There might even be a club history if the organisation was a long-lasting one, as well as, if the organisation no longer exists, papers about its dissolution.

Business records can include archives about production, sales, employees, shares, order book, advertising and promotional material, journals, accounts and minutes. There might be a company history.

These archives will vary in quantity. There might be relatively long and unbroken runs of minutes and other documentation, or they may be patchy. Although it is possible that these records may refer directly to ancestors, especially if they were strongly involved, perhaps as a senior committee member who played an important part in the life of the organisation, the only record might be your ancestor's name and address and start/finishing dates of their membership/employment.

This information will only merit a line in your family history notes and so the archive itself might seem to be of very minimal value. But its value is that it will help you understand about an aspect of their life. Reading the documents which correspond with your ancestor's association with the organisation will give insights into their time there, with an idea of the activities of the organisation with which they were probably involved. Of course, care needs to be taken here. Just because there was a dinner dance at the club pavilion on a certain date, it does not necessarily mean that your ancestor attended. They may well have done, but perhaps they were unwell or had another engagement elsewhere or were unable to attend.

Personal Archives
The personal records of individuals can also be found in some local archives. These can include correspondence, diaries and, very commonly, deeds to properties. Correspondence and diaries often contain very personal information which may be of little interest to anyone else. For instance, Henry St John who boarded at Acacia Road in Acton in the 1950s obsessively recorded the trivia of his existence, such as having lost his toothbrush, bemoaning his landlady's culinary shortcomings and being annoyed at a fellow lodger having his TV set on at a loud volume at night time. Not very interesting perhaps, unless one takes the view that one's own ancestor who was in lodgings might have had similar problems.

Alexander Kay Goodlet wrote in his diary on 13 February 1935:

Made a poor start and after breakfast returned to bed, so was not much help in the house till a late hour. The fact is I have a very bad cold and a damned sore chest, and that makes one a little slow.

Miss Heath and Joan and Thomasina were here to tea. Afterward I went up to Hanger Lane bridge and saw the

'Cheltenham Flyer' go through, the first time for months. Incidentally, was horrified to find large blocks of flats erected close to the District Railway; they must have gone up astonishingly quickly.

Later went to the Aunts' and to Ealing. Met Peggy M. on the way back. Went to dinner with Kidd and Joan and spent a most pleasant evening. Kidd and I discussed yachting rules exhaustively.

I see that the U.S. Navy airship 'Macon' is wrecked in the Pacific. Two lives lost out of 83.

Very informative about the life of the diarist, but not very useful for the history of the wider community.

No, the real interest in such private papers is the light they show on wider issues that confronted a locality or a nation at the time in question. Samuel Pepys's diary entries for 1666 give a unique insight into the experience of Londoners during the Great Fire, for instance. It is always worth finding out if any diaries or letters for a particular district coincide with your ancestor's life there, and if so they are worth reading. They are of even greater value if that diarist/correspondent has points in common with your ancestor, the same politics/religion/age/occupation/social class/sex and so on, because they may have had a similar outlook to that of your ancestor. Not necessarily of course; not everyone who is working class votes Labour, for instance and not all Catholics rigidly adhere to the doctrines of their church.

Attitudes expressed in diaries and letters are not necessarily those shared universally. Diaries and letters written during the Second World War show a variety of emotions. There is fear, there is stoicism and bravery and there is anger. Alexander Goodlet, the Ealing diarist in the 1930s just quoted, notes his dismay at the appeasement policies of the Chamberlain government at Munich in 1938. Yet this was not a popular position in Britain at that time, with most relieved (in the short term) of the need to face imminent death and destruction by bombing raids (as highlighted in the local press at the time).

Property Records
Deeds often exist in local repositories in great numbers. Until the late twentieth century it was necessary to produce deeds in great number

Sir,

I have conditionally bought of Mr Algood of Usk, a very improveable Estate in the Parish of Lanvrechva in the County of Monmouth, for the Use of the Church of Penterry in the Said County, provided the Governors of Queen Ann's Bounty will approve of the Conditions. The Purchase Money is to be two Hundred Pounds, and the Title, I am informed, is very good; for there was a Fine pass'd when the Purchase was made by Algood's Father, about forty Years ago. The Farm is let at present for no more than eight Pounds per Annum, and will at a very small Expence let for eleven Pounds, besides a Coppice Wood of three Years Growth, which at last Cutting was sold for twelve Guineas. I should therefore be very glad if the Bishop of Landaff would be pleas'd to send down a Commission, and whatever else is necessary, in Order to compleat the Purchase; I remain Sir, your most Obedient humble Servant

Tintern near Monmouth
December 20 1765

John Williams

Letter relating to a purchase of an estate, 1765. (Paul Lang)

in order to proceed with a property transaction and so individuals and solicitors often retained every deed relating to a property, often going back decades or even centuries. This is no longer necessary and so many deed collections have been passed by solicitors and others to record repositories (many have been destroyed or sold, however). Deeds mention individuals, of course, chiefly the buyer/tenant and seller/landlord, with their addresses and possibly occupations, along with other parties, such as spouses or family members or business partners.

Their real value lies in the details they give of a property, which may no longer be in existence. If your ancestors were involved in this property in whatever capacity (perhaps by renting it), they are of obvious interest. The deed will usually recount exactly what is in the property, house and grounds or flat, usually with dimensions and possibly a block plan. It should also recount the previous deeds to the property and so give the reader a brief history of the property and its changing hands over the years.

Deeds only exist for a minority of properties. But if your ancestors lived in London, Middlesex or Yorkshire from the early eighteenth to the early twentieth centuries, there are registries of deeds held at the London Metropolitan Archives, Wakefield Archives (for the West Riding of Yorkshire, what has been since 1974 West and South Yorkshire) and North Yorkshire Record Office for the North Riding). These provide abstracts of deeds and can be accessed by indexes, usually organised by year and then by the name of the seller.

Religious Archives
Religious bodies are also important even after the role of the Anglican Church in local government and testamentary administration faded away in the nineteenth century. Parish vestries had less work to do, but were still active in administering parish charities and acting as an advisory body and as a public forum on local issues. By the early twentieth century, they had been replaced by parochial church councils (not to be confused with parish councils, which are wholly secular bodies), whose sole remit was church affairs. Record of churches' Sunday Schools, youth clubs and women's fellowships can be also of great interest in recording the life of the church and its people. We should also remember that each parish is part of a large diocese, which

also creates records, including visitation records which are inspections of activity in each parish.

Protestant nonconformist and Catholic churches were not part of the Anglican administrative hierarchy of the sixteenth to the nineteenth century. Yet they were churches which had loyal congregations. And more importantly, they kept records. Catholic churches belong to dioceses, just as Anglican ones do, but nonconformity was variously organised. Methodist chapels are organised into circuits of chapels and were run by trustees. Their records include those of trustees, leaders, youth groups, treasurers and building, and can include minutes, plans, deeds, AGM records and many more which give an insight into the operation of these institutions.

Archives can be located by using the very useful Discovery website (once access to archives) hosted by the invaluable The National Archives website. This is a database of archives in English and Welsh archives, including the contents of The National Archives, which is annually updated. Searches can be made by name of organisation and can be further defined by geographical location and/or by name of repository. Archives are listed by type of record and date ranges for each one, down to item level (a term meaning an individual document, such as a minute book or a file of correspondence). Repositories often have their collections catalogued by archives software such as CALM and these are usually available online, on the archive's website. Searching by organisation as well as name can save much time by highlighting the whereabouts of potentially relevant information.

They should also note any restrictions on the accessibility of the said archives. Relatively recent material, anything from the early twentieth century onwards, may be closed due to concerns about the confidentiality of information contained therein. Court registers from the 1950s, for instance, are usually closed at present. Or documents might be closed because they are too fragile and need (often expensive) conservation work. Or they may be temporarily inaccessible due to storage issues. It is always worth enquiring about these items in case they can be made accessible at some stage in the future. A Freedom of Information request may also bear fruit.

Finally, do not forget that many archives, often dating back to the nineteenth century and beyond, are still held by the institution or organisation which created them. Schools and churches have often

Exterior of an eighteenth-century letter. (Paul Lang)

deposited their archives in a recognised place of deposit, but many have not done so, and so it is always worth contacting a place to see whether they have the archives sought and whether they can be viewed.

Archives are unique. Whereas many copies of a newspaper, a map, a book or a postcard are created, there will only be one minute book for the Blankshire Public Health Committee for 1920–4. So the information contained therein will be found nowhere else. Archives have their limitations due to imperfect knowledge and bias. Yet they were written at the time of events or very shortly afterwards by those immediately involved in them. So a reaction to a particular event may well be more accurate than in a memoir or account written years later, often with posterity in mind and with the benefit of hindsight. The contents of local repositories are essential to any passing study of local and family history.

Chapter 7

THE NATIONAL AND REGIONAL REPOSITORIES

Although the local archives are the obvious place to begin searching for local history, the researcher must remember that there are other archives which contain much about local history, but are often viewed solely as sources for national and international history. There are also some archives – a minority – which cover several counties or even the whole country. But they also cover local history, in part because they existed prior to the county archives of the twentieth century.

The National Archives
The National Archives at Kew is probably the UK's best known repository of archives and is certainly the biggest. It is the record office to central government, with archives dating from the eleventh century onwards, and has been since 1838 when it was founded as the Public Record Office on Chancery Lane in London (closed in 1996 and then entirely relocated at Kew). As a source for international and national history its treasures are immense and its researchers come from throughout the country and from overseas. It is well known and well used by both academic researchers, but mostly by family historians, especially those whose ancestors were in government employ, particularly in the armed forces in the past two centuries. What perhaps is not always realised that it is a great source for local history, too.

This is because government departments collected and collect information about people and places, and because events of important concern to the government must happen somewhere, often far from the central seat of power in Westminster. This has been the case since the time of The National Archives' oldest document, the Doomsday Book of 1086. These records are organised by the government department which created and collected them, not by locality. It is worth

The National Archives, 2015. (Author)

finding out information from other sources, perhaps books as a starter, about a locality, to learn where, how and when government policy and action had an impact on that district. Possibly there was an inquiry into a disaster or controversy. Or the National Archives' website can be searched by place, and then by date or/and government department.

One major series of records is the State Papers (SP) Domestic, which range from 1509 to 1783, and are the surviving correspondence to and from the Secretaries of State, who were the principal ministers of the crown until they were replaced by the Home and Foreign Offices, and are divided by the monarch's reign for the years which they cover. Those writing to them often had information about people, places and events in their localities which they thought should be brought to the attention of central authority. The letters deal with finance and trade, religious policy, law and order, and such important events such as the dissolution of the monasteries, the civil wars and the Jacobite rebellions. Although letters are the major part of these documents, they also include petitions, draft memoranda, orders in council, reports and newsletters.

The following extract from the State Papers for the reign of Charles II, dated 16 December 1674, reveals serious concerns about a religious minority and its impact on law and order in Yarmouth. The letter was written by Richard Bower and reads as follows:

Our nonconformists here now meet as formerly in their public place and in as great numbers, the people here being scared with letters they pretend they have got from the King and persuading the people that the Court were generally for their meeting, and only the Bishop endeavoured to oppose it. Notwithstanding these stories 2 or 3 citizens of Norwich went to their granary where there is an Independent and a Presbyterian meeting house, taking with them a constable to put them by, but coming into the Presbyterian meeting, they were set upon in the house, and had not Mr Barnham, one of the chief of them, rescued them out of their hands, they had there murdered them. However, before they were rescued, one of them was so beaten that he now lies in a sad condition. Our straits fleet are all sailed for the Downs to their convoy.

Following the creation of the Home Office, a new range of archives began to be generated by that, from 1782 to 1959 under the designation HO. This dealt with similar issues to the State Papers: law and order, public order, civil defence and so forth. The Privy Council (PC2), an advisory board to the monarch of principal politicians and others, also dealt with numerous local and national issues and these volumes are indexed.

The papers relating to the Assizes in England and Wales (up to the end of their existence in 1971) are also held here. Apart from being of obvious use to those with criminal ancestors, they can also provide an impression of the nature of relatively serious offences which were being tried at any one time in a particular locality, as do the Metropolitan Police files for the Greater London area from 1829 onwards.

The Parliamentary Archives

Parliamentary Papers are a key, but underused source for local history. They cover the last two centuries and are composed of numerous reports. These vary in size but cover topics in which the government of the day was interested. Poverty, workhouses, crimes, churches, taxation, schooling, farming and industry, transport and trade unions to name a few. They may include statistics and detailed evidence about these topics taken by inspectors and surveyors in the provinces. The British Library and Parliamentary Archives, once the House of Lords Records Office, have complete sets, incomplete sets may be held in reference libraries and university libraries, or be available on microfiche. There are also indexes available.

The archives at the Parliamentary Archives in Victoria Tower, viewable at the record office alongside the tower, date from 1497 (medieval parliamentary archives are held at the National Archives). The record office was established in 1946. It was once said that 'no general description can explain the wealth of detail often to be found' there, and most subjects from the last few centuries of British history can be found here. Initially, researchers working on the history of Parliament were the first to exploit the rich collection, but the scope has expanded vastly since then.

Most of the archives are of the Lords, since the archives of the Commons were destroyed when the Commons burnt down in 1834. The Acts of Parliament are the obvious archives held there. Some are of great national significance such as the Bill of Rights of 1689. Most are highly relevant to local and personal history, however, and deal with places throughout the country. These include parliamentary enclosure, the construction or repair of bridges and roads, divorce, naturalisation and other issues. All of these were Private Acts, initiated by individuals not the government, and do not deal with matters relating to the whole country. Most of these Private Acts survive in manuscript form, and few are printed for the period 1497–1797. These records are on parchment rolls up to 1850 and then in vellum books. However, most have been printed for the last two centuries. Unlike some documents written prior to 1733, they are in English with occasional French phrases. Where two versions exist, both printed and manuscript, it is always tempting to read the former, but the latter often contains material which is absent from the former.

One Act which was passed in 1795 was the following:

AN ACT To continue the Term, and enlarge the Powers of Two Acts, made in the Seventh and Thirty First Years of the Reign of His Present Majesty, for repairing the Highways from that Part of Counter's Bridge which lies in the Parish of Kensington, in the County of Middlesex, leading through the Towns of Brentford and Hounslow to the Powder Mills in the Road to Staines, and to Cranford Bridge in the said County, in the Road to Colnbrook; and for repairing, turning or altering the Highway leading from the said Road, at or near the End of Sion Lane, to the Town of Isleworth in the said County, and from thence to a Gate on the South side of Teddington Field; and also the Highway leading out of the said Great Road near Smallberry-Green Turnpike, to a House known by the Sign of the George in the Town of Isleworth aforesaid; and for lighting and watering Part of the said Highways.

Apart from the Acts, there is other relevant material. These are Bills, Proceedings and Petitions. Journals of the two Houses show the progress of a Bill through them. Cobbett's *Parliamentary History* covers the seventeenth and eighteenth centuries. From 1803 Hansard covered the debates. Petitions, which proceed Bills, often reveal the plight of communities whose livelihood was perhaps in danger and who needed legislation to protect it. Or there may be petitions calling for religious or political reform. When Catholic Emancipation was discussed in the 1820s, 20,000 petitions were sent to Parliament, from numerous towns throughout the country, showing that many people were concerned over religious issues at this time.

There is also a large collection of maps and plans here. This is because many Private Bills concern particular localities, especially the enclosure bills and those establishing public works. They can include plans for railway and canal routes. Scales of maps are variable; from 2 inches to 24 to the mile. Many predate the Ordnance Survey maps, so can be a very valuable source of maps for earlier centuries.

Committee proceedings, especially from 1800, include transcriptions of the evidence given before Lords' and Commons' committees. For a Bill in 1835 about traffic on the Thames, evidence was given about the employment of watermen, about the state of the poor in the parish, the growth of the town of Gravesend. Witnesses included the humblest of men. Local knowledge was provided by local inhabitants and was recorded in these documents.

The British Library
Another relevant repository is the British Library, which does not only contain books (and newspapers as explained in Chapter 5). It holds a major collection of manuscripts, too, from the Middle Ages onwards. These include letters, antiquarian collections and other papers deposited there since the eighteenth century by politicians, writers and others, many of national importance. The manuscripts' database allows searching by place name and so it is a speedy job to ascertain whether there is anything worth examining there. For example, when researching for a history of Acton in Middlesex, I found a relevant

The British Library, 2014. (Author)

reference in Additional Manuscripts 61619. It told of a petition to Queen Anne in 1707. Apparently at 'the west end of the town of Acton near the gravel pits, between the road and the footpath' there swung the remains of a hanged arsonist in a gibbet. The parish's inhabitants were concerned that 'the smell of him is become very nauseous and offensive to your petitioners and all persons passing and repairing that road'. Regrettably the outcome of the petition is unknown, but this information is unique and casts a light on life in the parish at that time.

Ecclesiastical Archives and Libraries

Lambeth Palace Library, in central London, has, since 1610, housed the library of the archbishopric of Canterbury, which is one of the oldest public libraries in the world. It is the principal record office for the archbishopric of Canterbury and for the Church of England, as well as housing an extensive library of printed material. Its collections date from the ninth century to the twenty-first. Readers do not need an appointment but they do need proof of identity to obtain a reader's ticket.

For local and family historians, perhaps the most important aspect of the library is the fact that the Church of England was and is a large property owner. Land was bought in order to provide clergymen with an income and so most parishes included some, known as glebe land. Cathedrals also bought land, too. In the nineteenth century, much of this land was sold and the money invested elsewhere. The archives contain a great deal of information about these properties. These include maps and correspondence relating to estate management, new buildings, drainage and other matters concerning the land in question.

Much of the holdings of the archbishopric consisted of land in Kent, Surrey and Middlesex, but there were smaller landholdings throughout the country. Documents for these include leases and registers of the church's holdings there. Under the Commonwealth (1649–60) the church lost its lands to the state, which sold some of these lands or administered them itself. Surveys were undertaken in 1649–50 and 1655–6 and these are held at the library. Church properties were administered by the Ecclesiastical Commissioners from 1862, and among these files are papers relating to estate management, local agricultural and industry, markets, customs and other material.

There are also visitation records. These were surveys of the parishes taken every seven years at the behest of the archbishop. These considered spiritual matters in the parish, but also educational concerns and the state of the church fabric, too.

The Lambeth Palace Library website is the best place for any would-be researcher to begin with. It includes a large number of research guides. These include guides to church architectural history, family history, local history, church property, educational history and clergy history.

Although most of these national repositories are in or near London, there are significant collections elsewhere outside the network of county and borough archives and libraries. One is the Borthwick Institute, which is part of York University and is housed on the main campus about a mile from the city centre. This is, inter alia, the diocesan record office for the archbishopric and diocese of York (the equivalent of Lambeth Palace for the southern archbishopric). Records of church properties taken over by the ecclesiastical commissioners in the nineteenth century are also held here. Anyone interested in the history of the people of Yorkshire should not ignore this repository.

Although the core of the holdings are diocesan and archiepiscopal, there are also records of Catholic and nonconformist churches in or near York. Records of York hospitals from 1740 onwards are located here; such as those of the York Lunatic Asylum from 1777 and the county hospital from 1740. There are also records of schools, charities, businesses (such as Rowntrees and Terry's). There are family papers, the most nationally significant being of the Wood family of the Earls of Halifax. All these accrued to the Institute because it predated the county record offices in this part of Yorkshire and so institutions and families deposited their papers here; its prestige encouraged later depositors.

An example of an archiepiscopal record is the following, ordering clergy to relay to their parishioners in church the necessity for obedience to their King and government following the rebellion known as the Pilgrimage of Grace in 1536:

Briane the dean of the metroplitain churche of Yorke and the chapter of the same to the curates in the back of this letter written send greting in our lord god euerlasting. This ys to aduertise you that w ehaue receyuid a commaundment frome my lord Archebusshop of Yorke concerning publishing and declaracion of certain articles as hereafter ensew. Therefore by the auctoryte of the same commaundment we command you to declare the same euery sundaie or other tymes in yor sermondes and bidding of headdes and instruct yor parochianors after the forme and maner following:

Furst shew theim that ther dutie by the commaundment of god ys to be obedient to our souerain lord the king and in no wise to disobaie or rebel against is laws ordinances or other in any thing his comaundementes.

Also that the late insurreccion and disobedience against his maiesti was deadly synne and for the same mortall offence they be bound to make amendes towards both god and his maiestie for the dischagyng of their sowles and that they attempt not hereafter any like mortall offence.

Also that you exort them both in confessions and otherwise to conforme them selfes in all pointes to such order as it shall pleas the kings highness to take for the gouernance and quietnes of this his realme. Also we send to you a booke concerning other articles as doth appere in the same which you shall declare or at the least sum parte therof euery sundaie in the polepitt in the presens of yor parochianers or the more parte therof and so contynew in the same tyll you haue ferder commaundment from the kings highness or by ys. And that ye faill not herein as yet will therto answer at yor uttermost perell yevin under our seal the xiiii daie of February the yere of our lord god 1536.

University Archives and Libraries

Before the advent of record offices and libraries, there were the university libraries. Perhaps the greatest of these is the Bodleian Library at Oxford, inaugurated in 1612. This is the first library of deposit in England, with a right to possess a copy of each book published in England. Its collection of Western Manuscripts is the second largest in the country. It includes papers of Oxford antiquarians such as Thomas Hearne and Anthony Wood (active in the eighteenth and seventeenth centuries), as well as later local historians. There are also estate papers of important families such as the Harcourts, Dashwoods and Norths. Some of the colleges have deposited their manuscripts there. Its map

The new Bodleian Library, 2014. (Author)

collection has already been noted in Chapter 4. Although this is the principal library of the university, it can be accessed by the public, though a fee is payable for a membership card.

Other university archives (especially the older ones) should not be neglected either. University libraries do not only hold books and journals for use of the student body, but many have special collections of material which will probably never be seen or even thought of by the bulk of the undergraduate population. University libraries collect the archives of their parent body and some of these archives, for the ancient universities, date back to the Middle Ages. These can include documents relating to the properties owned by the colleges; often at great distance from the university itself.

More recent universities often have special collections, albeit of a more recent pedigree. The libraries of Hull and Huddersfield universities hold much that is relevant to labour unrest, trade unions and working-class politics, for example.

Another national repository is the Modern Records Centre, based at Warwick University Library from 1973. It holds, principally, the archives of trade unions (and that of the TUC), but also of some employers' associations and political pressure groups. These archives date back to the eighteenth century. Trade unions create annual returns of their activities and accounts, often broken up by branch level. Minutes of conferences also exist. These records help shed a light on the wages and working conditions of men and women employed in various unionised trades and industries, and their attempts to improve their conditions of work. Information can be found about industrial action that can be supplemented from oral history accounts if they exist and also from the press, sympathetic and hostile to the unions' activities.

There are two major repositories in Manchester which deserve special mention, too, because of their regional significance. These are

Interior of Bodleian Library. (Paul Lang)

Chetham's Library and the John Rylands Library (the latter is part of Manchester University). Chetham's was founded in the seventeenth century and so is one of the oldest public libraries in the world. Although the John Rylands lacks such a pedigree (established in 1900), both institutions were founded before county and borough record offices were in existence. This meant that both were collecting not only books but important archive collections at a relatively early era.

Between 1921 and 1940 the John Rylands Library appealed to the local gentry to deposit their archives with them and this resulted in the acquisition of over 20 family collections dating from the Middle Ages to the twentieth century. Both libraries have many archives pertaining to both Lancashire and Cheshire in particular, but also have material relevant to Derbyshire, Lincolnshire and Shropshire and elsewhere. These archives include manorial records, rentals, archives of land tenure and use. There are also the collections of antiquarian collectors and much more. One particularly interesting item at Chetham's is the diary of Edmund Harrold, an early eighteenth-century Manchester wigmaker. Papers relevant to Manchester politics and industries also feature in these collections. Both places also have significant collections of books, prints, pamphlets of relevance to the northwest of England.

These libraries and record offices are not obvious sources of local history and would not be the first port of call. Their online catalogues should be consulted prior to a visit to determine whether there is any material of potential interest. The National Archives is the most important institution, but regional repositories should be investigated, too.

Chapter 8

FIELDWORK

Professor Hoskins, a great populariser of local history and the first head of the newly established department of Local History at Leicester University, once observed that, even if there was a catastrophe in which all the contents of libraries and archives were destroyed, it would still be possible to conduct historical research as long as the researcher had use of their feet and eyes. Thankfully we do not have to contemplate such an apocalyptic scenario, but to restrict one's research to reading documents and looking at information on microfilm or on a computer screen indoors is a restriction that need not be contemplated. He also commented: 'You may ransack every source you can think of, printed and manuscript, in all conceivable record offices in England and in your own district: but this is by no means the end of the story.' Open-air observation is strongly recommended. Anyone who does so is following in the footsteps of many local historians from the Middle Ages onwards, who took delight in making tours in order to gather the necessary information for their written work.

An important series of books will be useful here as guides. These are the architectural surveys of extant buildings (at time of writing) by Nicholas Pevsner and his successors (*Buildings of England*; *Buildings of Scotland*). Each covers a single county, though some are subdivided into two or more volumes, and some have been renamed in line with changes in local government – there is no new Middlesex volume, for instance, and some may take a city as their subject. First published in the 1950s and the 1960s by the man himself, there have been more recent (expanded and updated) volumes in the 1990s and 2000s by his successors. These have been far more wide-ranging in coverage of buildings and are no longer restricted to major public buildings, ancient buildings and churches. They give details of architect if applicable, dates and key features and alterations of buildings which were extant at time of writing. The books are generously provided with photographs and maps. Although these books can be expensive to buy, they can often be borrowed from libraries.

Put simply, the task of a survey should probably be undertaken after some of the more traditional research has been undertaken (and on a dry day, so photographs can be taken and buildings viewed leisurely). You should already have a knowledge of which address(es) your ancestors lived in, the school(s) they attended, the church they worshipped at, where they worked and perhaps where they undertook their leisure activities. Armed with these, a detailed modern map, and perhaps an older one (one of the Godfrey edition, perhaps), as well as a camera, you can then visit the place where your ancestors lived.

Walk the streets, use your maps and identify these places. Try and locate them. Photograph them. If the buildings are open to the public go inside, perhaps on Open House weekend (late September; check which buildings are open and when, also to see whether booking is required). Perhaps they belong to the National Trust or English Heritage. If they are churches, try making an appointment with the minister or churchwardens for access (or go when the building is open). Of course, with buildings which are private, prior contact is advisable and if you are fortunate, you may be allowed to visit. When researching for a biography recently I contacted the current owners of my subject's childhood home, and was pleased that the present occupiers both knew about the former resident (acid bath murderer John George Haigh) in question and invited me to visit. Another researcher I know once visited the house they were interested in in the guise of a prospective buyer, the property then being for sale.

Industrial heritage is another matter. Whilst there is relatively little industry in Britain in the early twenty-first century, industry was a major part of the economy in the nineteenth century and for much of its successor. It was also important in other centuries, too. Mining occurred in the Middle Ages and subsequent centuries. Traces of old tin mines are recognisable in the southwest. From the seventeenth to the twentieth century the textile industry was dominant in Lancashire and the West Riding of Yorkshire.

An instant objection to this line of enquiry may be that times and districts change. Indeed they do; for example, in South Acton, part of the London Borough of Ealing in west London, rows of late nineteenth-century terraced houses were swept away after 1945 by tower blocks.

The numerous laundries which existed there (205 in 1900) have also disappeared so that a local historian once observed that one would be more surprised to see a laundry there than a dinosaur.

It is true that many houses from previous centuries have been demolished, often because they were deemed unfit for human habitation, so were compulsorily purchased as part of schemes of slum clearance in the twentieth century. Yet it is rare for every single house to have been destroyed. Often some houses or even whole terraces, perhaps better built or in better condition than others, were retained as being satisfactory or capable of being improved. Ironically, in some cases, the housing which replaced them is being demolished in turn, after having lasted for a shorter period of time than those which initially stood there.

Or buildings may still stand but have been partitioned or are being used for other purposes. The former is often the case with the larger Victorian dwellings, initially built for a single household, with a number of servants and at a time when energy and other costs were relatively inexpensive. They often had spacious grounds. The later twentieth century led to the demise in this form of household and so a reduced demand for the housing it engendered. In some cases, of course, the houses have been demolished and new ones, or flats, built in their place. Or the property is now several residences, with the grounds sometimes built on as well, such is the demand for housing to meet the current population expansion. Or such houses are now used for non-residential purposes, such as a school.

Buildings have changed uses in other ways. Schools in the eighteenth and early nineteenth century, before compulsory education, were often houses in which the schoolmaster once lived. Some redundant churches have been converted into other uses. Although many industrial buildings have ceased to exist, some still do and have been converted for other uses. For example, Dean Clough Mill, which was a major employer in nineteenth- and twentieth-century Halifax, has been converted into small workshops, whilst the exterior has been more or less preserved. Likewise, Halifax's eighteenth-century Piece Hall, once a major market for textiles, still stands, but is now used by many small businesses and shops.

Military buildings should also be considered. Ancestors who served in the armed forces, Home Guard or militia may well have been stationed in barracks or forts throughout Britain. Thousands of pillboxes, for example, were built on the coastline and elsewhere and you may have discovered that your ancestor manned them, waiting to repel an invasion which never came. Or perhaps they were in the regular forces and were stationed in a major fortification such as Fort Augustus, near Inverness, which though still in use by the military (as it has been since the eighteenth century) is mostly open to the public.

A number of the great country houses, including those still in private hands, such as Syon House, in London, are open to the public for an entry price. It may be objected that most of our ancestors did not own such mansions. But servants' quarters and kitchens beneath stairs are a major feature of these places, and, with the popularity of dramas such as *Downton Abbey*, are increasingly of interest and relevance.

It is not just the grand buildings like Castle Howard, Blenheim Palace and Basildon Park which can be viewed as a matter of course. Open-air

Kitchen of Audley End, 2014. (Author)

museums, such as Beamish in the north of England and the Chiltern Open Air Museum in Buckinghamshire, are comprised of ordinary domestic buildings, including a toll house of the eighteenth century, prefabs of the 1940s and farmyard barns. Some of these buildings, or at least part of them, are designated as museums, with period furniture, explanation boards and informative guides.

Even buildings which are still used for their original purpose, such as some of the older public schools, the older Oxbridge colleges, cathedrals and churches, for instance, are not unchanged. Internal as well as external building fabric has often changed. A medieval church, where ancestors were wed in the sixteenth century (as ascertained from the parish registers) and which was not rebuilt by Gilbert Scott in the nineteenth century, will not have remained the same over time. There may have been damage caused by the Puritans in the seventeenth century; medieval wall paintings whitewashed during the sixteenth-century reformation may have been revealed in the nineteenth; pews may have been replaced by chairs or reduced in number in the twentieth century. A perusal of the church history or the appropriate entry in Pevsner's architectural guide should indicate the alterations over time. They should also explain the features which were extant at the time of your ancestors, and which they would have known.

For those whose ancestors spent time in a workhouse, the preserved workhouse at Southwell in Nottinghamshire, now cared for by the National Trust, may be worth seeing. It was built in 1824 and was a model for later structures. There is also the Workhouse Museum at Gressenhall, Norfolk.

There have been a number of laws passed to prevent historic buildings from being demolished (former ages had no such compunction about the demolition of older buildings to make way for newer ones). In 1877 the Society for the Preservation of Ancient Buildings was founded and in 1882 the first relevant piece of legislation was passed. This was the Ancient Monuments Protection Act and listed 29 buildings in England and 21 in Scotland that were now protected by law. A further Act in 1913 created the Ancient Monuments Board which had inspectors and commissioners to list buildings of national importance. They also recorded other significant buildings, which were not deemed of national importance but were still worthy of protection. The Historic Buildings and Monuments Act of 1931 enabled the

Ministry of Works to issue immediate preservation notices on the recommendation of the previously exiting boards.

Powers were devolved on local government with the 1944 Town and Country Planning Act. In each local government district there was drawn up a list of historically important buildings classified by grade. Grade I buildings were those of such importance that they should never be destroyed; they are rare. Grade II* are more common, and are not to be demolished without very good reason. There are also Grade II buildings, which have less protection. However, such protection can be revoked and so demolition can then go ahead – this often happens where buildings are decayed and the necessary renovation would be so expensive that destruction seems the lesser evil. Lists of such buildings should be available on the website of county and borough councils. Some listings also list additional buildings or groups of buildings which are seen as being of value but are not statutorily listed. By 2015 there were 376,099 listed buildings in England and Wales.

Whitchurch Silk Mill, Hampshire, 2014. (Author)

Industrial buildings were added to the list of potentially protected structures in 1953 and in 1962 an Act was passed enabling local authorities to make grants for the protection of such buildings. A new definition of what could be preserved was created in 1979 with the Ancient Monuments and Archaeological Areas Act. This made it possible for almost any building to be deemed historic and worthy of protection.

In 1967 the Conservation Act led to local authorities being able, if they wished, to designate a number of districts in their jurisdiction as conservation zones. Sometimes local groups, often residents' associations or conservation societies, would petition their council to have a particular district given this status. Districts chosen often included obvious places such as the houses around village greens, but could also include innovative housing

Monumental inscription at St Peter's church, Iver, 2015. (Author)

developments of more recent times. This legislation gave protection to the buildings in that district and planning restrictions were tighter than elsewhere; for instance hedgerows and other key features could not be removed, and external changes to houses were limited.

Memorials in churches have an obvious interest to the family historian. But though very few people are represented by such memorials because of their cost, they are still of importance to those whose families were less affluent. They can often reveal much about local circumstances. For example in St Peter's church in Iver, Buckinghamshire, there is a memorial to 12 children who died between 1704 and 1720. This is symptomatic of the high rate of infant mortality, even among the relatively wealthy, at this time.

There are two major national organisations which do much to preserve the country's built heritage. These are the National Trust and

English Heritage. Both are charities dependent on donations and subscriptions of members and admission fees from others. The former was founded in 1895. Country houses built in the eighteenth and nineteenth centuries were being demolished in the post-Second World War years when families could no longer afford their upkeep. Fortunately these charities were able to acquire some of them, usually with endowments, from families who no longer wished – or were able – to own them. This gave them a new lease of life from tourists and also being used as backdrops for films and TV productions.

English Heritage was founded in 1983 as the government's statutory adviser on the historic environment, with 16 commissioners, and was advised by 13 specialist committees. It also served to advise local authorities on the management of their responsibilities and provided grants for the regeneration of places in need.

Their portfolios also include ruined castles and ecclesiastical buildings dating from the Middle Ages and beyond. It is important to remember that these preserved sites are very unrepresentative of the dwellings that our ancestors lived in. Most people resided in far more modest houses in towns and villages and these ordinary houses rarely survive or are still being lived in. For instance two twentieth-century suburban houses in Liverpool, childhood homes of John Lennon and Paul McCartney, were only acquired by the National Trust because of their former famous occupants.

Let us take a building that would have been central in your ancestors' lives for centuries: the parish church. Now, it is impossible to elbow our way into the past; the past is not an experiment that can be repeated.

St Peter's church in Iver would be described as a medieval church. Certainly there was a church on this site since the eleventh century. Yet it is not a museum and should be viewed as being an organic structure, which has features of many periods. On the north side of the nave there is a double splayed window with pinkish sandstone, which, as the former curate never tired as telling visitors and congregation alike, was late Saxon and the oldest visible part of the church. Much of the body of the church and tower is thirteenth century.

Yet many of the church's features are of other periods. The font is Norman, for instance. The pulpit, decorated with cherub heads and garlands, is seventeenth century. The stained glass is late Victorian and

St Peter's church, Iver, 2015. (Author)

Edwardian. The top of the tower is late medieval and the bells chiefly date from the eighteenth century. The monuments and memorials in the church are of a variety of dates. That of Richard Blount, in armour, with his family dates from 1508, and there is an early seventeenth-century memorial to John King, slain by a kinsman, Roger Parkinson. The vestry was added in the late 1890s and a century later a kitchen and social space was added next to it. There is the inevitable children's corner of toys, dating from recent years.

All this does not mean that a visit is worthless, but that the visitor should study their Pevsner in advance and be on their guard, realising that some of the church may well postdate their ancestors' knowledge of it. Generally speaking, exteriors are better preserved than interiors, but drastic alterations can and did occur; the remodelling of St Mary's church in Ealing in the mid-Victorian era has completely obscured the box Georgian church onto which a basilica was grafted.

Even towns and villages which might appear to have been wholly altered by radical changes in the twentieth century are not wholly lost causes as far as local and family history is concerned. Crawley, an apparently unprepossessing New Town of the 1950s, has kept its charming High Street, resplendent with centuries-old hostelries (one now an Italian chain restaurant) and parish church. It is not, therefore, just the 'historic' towns and cities (e.g. York, Chester, Oxford, etc.) in which the buildings of the past remain. Seek and ye might find.

Chapter 9

OTHER SOURCES

There is a myriad of other sources to be found in record offices which may be of use to the local historian as well as a family historian. These may be catalogued and the catalogues available electronically or the only finding aids may be a card catalogue system or even the archivist's own knowledge. The latter should never be underestimated, especially if they have worked at a particular institution for a lengthy period of time. Asking questions is always recommended.

Oral History
Oral history, which uses the reminiscences of people (often described as being 'ordinary') to shed a light on the past, has a long pedigree, though it was not named as such until the twentieth century. Since the sixteenth century historians have been talking to old men about the past. These 'stories' were first collected seriously in Britain at the end of the nineteenth century. An early book based on interviews was that by Diana Mulock in 1884, *An Unsentimental Journey through Cornwall*. George Evans's *Ask the Fellows Who Cut the Hay* in 1956 was another book based on interviews. In 1971 the journal, *Oral History*, was founded by the Oral History Society, based at Essex University, and they run courses and provide information for those contemplating undertaking such recording projects. These books and projects consist of interviews with people, often elderly, though not always. (Ealing's Polish Oral History project in 2009 recorded voices of people from their twenties to their seventies.)

The British Library holds numerous recordings of the spoken word, over a million discs, 185,000 tapes and many other video and sound recordings. Not all are relevant; some are of wildlife, some are from overseas, some are of music, drama and literature. Other recordings, which pertain to a particular district, are held in the relevant record offices, libraries and museums. Some recordings have been transcribed either in full or as synopses. In other cases it may be necessary to listen to the recordings; in any case, these can add a potency to even complete transcriptions. Some are available online; the Imperial War Museum has many recordings from service personnel and others. Some extracts have been published as books such as those mentioned in the preceding paragraph.

Oral history has had its critics. Professor A J P Taylor claimed it was merely old men telling tales. Some accounts of events may not be entirely based on memory but on interpretations taken from other sources. It certainly needs to be treated rigorously, just as any other source would be. Where possible, checks against other sources are needed, especially those made at the time. Clearly elderly people can be forgetful of incidents that happened decades ago, just as witnesses in trials months after a serious crime are usually severely cross-examined by the barrister of the opposing side. Yet memory of recent events may well be more suspect than that of long ago. On the other hand, not everything in history is written down and so the power of memory can help illuminate incidents that might otherwise be inexplicable.

The potential value of oral history is that it can unlock the history of a community in a way that no other source can. It can open up details of life and work that are not recorded elsewhere. Although there are books featuring extracts from oral history projects, which are usually based on a particular theme, locality or a certain time period or an industry, these are only the tip of the iceberg of work which lies behind them. The actual interviews will certainly be more thorough and potentially more valuable.

The value of Medical Officers' reports has been referred to in Chapter 2, but oral histories can put flesh on the bones of what would otherwise be mere statistics. The report will state how much infant mortality there was, but only in terms of numbers. As human beings it is easier to empathise with human stories. An elderly lady, recalling incidents from her childhood in Lancashire in the 1890s, stated:

I can remember her carrying that little coffin with the baby in. I often think about these girls that take babies. She said that every baby she saw she wanted to snatch. She would have stolen anybody's baby to fill that want. She had all those but she couldn't spare one.

Another interviewee responded:

> Then we buried Maggie May … she was the loveliest little thing
> that ever walked and she started with diptheria and I've heard my
> mother say that she rolled from the top of the bed to the bottom
> to get her breath. There was no immunization, no nothing.

Oral history is perhaps at its best when it describes, not generalities,
highlights and major events, but the day-to-day life of those interviewed.
What their daily routine was like, life at home, at work, experience of
religion and schooling. These are the issues which will tend to go
unreported by journalists and others, who are more concerned with
extraordinary events – an annual horticultural show rather than an
evening spent on the allotment or in the pub with friends.

An extract from the reminiscences gathered at Gunnersbury Park
Museum in the book, *Ealing and Hounslow Lives* (1999) from one Tom
Bowles in the late twentieth century, but looking back decades, is as
follows:

> We used to serve all Hayes and Southall with cargo and we used
> to take the sleepers, shiploads of sleepers for the Great Western
> Railway to lay on the tracks. We used to take sugar and oranges to
> Keeley and Toms which was a jam factory in Southall, sugar, cocoa
> beans and nuts to Nestle's milk factory at Hayes, timber to HMV,
> they used to make the gramophones and pianos and all that sort
> of thing. Timber to Uxbridge and Watford, wood pulp up to Croxley.
> Safety regulations came into it a lot. We used to have inspectors
> come down; trade unions had rules regarding lifting and all that
> sort of thing. You was only allowed to lift what you could lift, say
> there was two of us, we'd pick up a sack of wheat, say two hundred
> weight. You couldn't pick it up on your own. I've seen women on
> boats get hold of hundredweight boxes of sugar and tea and load
> them on their backs. One woman, a big woman she was, she used
> to say to her husband 'Come on let me have a go at that' and she'd
> push him out of the way and she'd get this bag of sugar and load
> it on the boat, she'd step down and just plant it. They could do it
> as good as men, 'cos they had to work as hard as men, those
> women on the boats, had to work very hard, all hours, all night.

LONDON CEMETERY COMPANY,

Incorporated by Act of Parliament 6 & 7 Wm. IV. c. 136.

DIRECTORS.

The Rev. J. RUSSELL, D.D. Chairman.—BENJ. HAWES, Esq. Dep. Chairman

JAMES ANDERTON, Esq.   WILLIAM SAMUEL JONES, Esq.
MICHAEL JOSEPH BLOUNT, Esq.   THOMAS BRIDGE SIMPSON, Esq.
Major CHARLES LESTOCK BOILEAU.   JONAH SMITH WELLS. Esq.
                GEORGE HAMMOND WHALLEY, E

AUDITORS.

The Rev. J. W. VIVIAN, D.D. | O. B. BEL

HIGHGATE CEMETERY OF

Office, 21, NEW BRIDGE STREET, BL

BURIAL of *William Frederick Boyle*

Residence *Halliford Street, Islington*

at *11* o'clock, on *Tuesday* the *5* of *June* 185*5*

	£	s.	d
Catacomb Compartment			
Tablet			
Public Vault			
Ground for Brick Grave			
Brickwork			
For a Private Grave, 7 feet deep . . 6½ by 2½ *over which a Monument or Grave Stones must be erected in 12 months*			
Extra Depth of Grave to feet..			
Extra Ground to a			
Opening and re-closing			
Moving and re-placing Monument or Grave Stone			
A Common Interment in a Grave (*no Stone allowed*)	3	3	.
Inscription			
Fees on Interment			
Maintaining Grave			
Entry of Grant			
Service before Two o'clock		7	6
Turfing Grave			
Iron Bearers			
5 day of *June* 185*5* £	3	10	6

EDW. BUXTON, SECRETARY & REGISTRAR.

Highgate Cemetery certificate, 1855. (Paul Lang)

Ephemera

Ephemera are another form of historical source which may now be of the utmost value, but at the time may well have been deemed by some to be of merely temporary worth and so would not naturally be kept for posterity. They are items that do not fit easily into any other classification. These are handwritten or printed papers which were not meant to be kept forever, but have accrued at record offices. They may include cuttings from magazines and newspapers, advertising materials, invoices and bills, tickets, electioneering matter, estate agents' adverts, as well as leaflets from other organisations and much more. A recent piece of ephemera which was handed into my place of work was an illustrated brochure for a housing development in what was then rural Greenford. The virtues of the houses and the location are extolled. A plan of the house is shown, as well as relevant fees and other prices. Two veteran local historians were shown this and were particularly excited about this item which was new to them. There is even an *Encyclopedia of Ephemera*, published in 2000, and which may be of use and can often be found in reference libraries.

These are often organised thematically; perhaps by locality or perhaps by type of information or perhaps by subject matter. This often includes such wide categories as crime, famous people, housing, immigration, parks and open spaces, transport and politics. These items may be indexed online or in other ways, or they may resemble the lucky dip of a bran tub.

One example of a scrapbook, created by a man with a strong interest in local history, was that of Montague Jones, whose family had lived in Ealing since the early nineteenth century. He created a book of cuttings, mostly dating from the 1940s and 1950s. These were taken from the local newspaper, *The Middlesex County Times*. They included letters written by him and published there, as well as letters on the same topics but from others, and articles which interested him. He wrote to give information to others, to correct them and often criticise the actions of the council. The book of cuttings has subsequently been indexed by library staff.

Trade tokens are another example of ephemera. Money was not the only form of currency in use from the seventeenth century to the nineteenth, such was the shortage of coin of the realm. Shopkeepers often issued trade tokens which could be used in their shops. Tens of

Advert for local football match. (Paul Lang)

thousands of businesses used such 'coinage' and they provide evidence for the existence of a variety of shops in the countryside and small towns. They were often illustrated.

Films

Another dimension for local and family historians is moving footage showing people and places in the past. Moving pictures first appeared in 1888. Perhaps the best known to many, because it was televised in three episodes with a commentary and interviews, and then made available on DVD is *The Lost World of Sagar Mitchell and James Kenyon*, two photographers in Blackburn in the first decade of the twentieth century. The films showed people in the streets, coming out from work, playing football, special processions, holidays, crime and many other events. The background to all this was the streets of Edwardian Blackburn, and transport also featured heavily. One point which might strike some viewers is that almost everyone is wearing a hat, in contrast to more recent decades.

Museums and some universities also hold a good deal of visual material. East Anglia University had films of holidays in the Norfolk Broads in the 1920s, fish quay scenes in Great Yarmouth in the 1900s, a swimming race at Ipswich in 1913 and farming in Suffolk in the 1930s. Local history societies also filmed their localities and events in the 1950s and 1960s and these now are of historical interest. A small film taken from the top deck of a tram along the Uxbridge Road shows pedestrians and cyclists as well as surrounding streets in the 1900s.

The advantage of these films is that they show the people of the past as people; 'real' people who move and are active, not just those who stand or sit stiffly in formal photographic portraits. It helps us to connect and identity with the past in a way that written words, as valuable as they are in many ways, do not always do.

The Internet

The internet is the first avenue of research for many people on many topics, and has been so for the past decade. It is, however, a very mixed bag – another lucky dip, perhaps. Wikipedia has a great number of articles about various towns, villages and counties, and these usually include historical information. Often this information is properly sourced, although the reliability of the sources can be questioned. Articles are usually very short compared to books on the topic. As with much information on the internet, it is probably best to take of note of what is relevant and then make a note to check it against other sources.

There are more reliable sources. Local history societies will have a website, as will county and borough record offices, as well as the National Archives. These are usually informative and reliable, written by those involved in the organisation itself. Information about holdings and events is usually given, as well as relevant illustrative matter and contact details for further information. Text of some books can also be found on the internet where a book (out of copyright) has been scanned in its entirety, such as the diary of Thomas Tyldesley, a Lancashire Catholic gentleman with a wide circle of friends who are often mentioned.

Trade token. (Paul Lang)

It is impossible to list every single source that has been preserved which might shed a light on local history. Different places have different sources of information. The question is to ask and see what there is. Surprises may be in store.

Chapter 10

MUSEUMS

Museums have existed since the seventeenth century in England; the Ashmolean Museum in Oxford being the first, with the British Museum following in the eighteenth century. Many more were created in the nineteenth and twentieth centuries throughout the country. Some are in public hands and some are owned privately. They are now seen as places of entertainment and discovery, rather than just as places of instruction and education which is how they were initially envisaged. Most towns and cities possess a museum. As with archives and libraries, some are of a national nature, for example, the National Army Museum (in London) or the National Museum of Media, Film and Photography (in Bradford). Some are centred around a particular type of collection, such as the Horniman Museum of natural history and ethnography in Forest Hill, or around a particular famous person, such as Apsley House, for the Duke of Wellington. Others, though, focus on the history of the locality. Some cover both particular subjects and the locality, such as the Museum of Rowing in Henley which covers the history of the town as well as that of the sport associated with it. These are of particular interest to the local and family historian.

County, city and town museums were originally the product of local municipal pride on the part of civic dignitaries, often to promote their town in comparison with neighbours and perhaps to increase tourism and local trade. Initially the collections were often haphazard and very esoteric. Stuffed birds and animals from Britain or elsewhere often featured, and other items collected from across the globe. Fossils and geological specimens were also included in these collections. This was because donations from the museum's backers and friends were almost obligatory. Museums may be exist in purpose-built buildings but many are in a part of a council-owned building, which may be a former mansion or other historic building (sometimes in its own grounds).

The key difference between museums and libraries/archives is that

Shop front in Horsham Museum, 2014. (Author)

the former are principally repositories of three-dimensional items, known as artefacts. There are usually other items as well, but artefacts are the primary components of the collection. Whereas most archives and libraries are free to use, many museums charge an entry fee, though there may be reductions for locals and season tickets are sometimes available. They are often open on Sundays and bank holidays, unlike the majority of archives and specialist libraries.

It is worth recalling that the exhibits in some museums predate those held in record offices and libraries. Museums often hold the archaeological remains of the district, which predate the written record by some centuries.

Until the late twentieth century almost all museum collections were located in glass cabinets or were roped off. Items there were to be seen and admired, not touched. This, of course, was for security and conservation as overhandling damages precious items. More recently, though, whilst these principles are not neglected, a more open attitude has been adopted. Often replicas are on open access and signs encourage their handling. Children, too, are often encouraged, and there are often parts of the museum specifically set aside for younger visitors, with appropriate toys and costumes. Film shows and audio tour guides are commonplace, too, and help guide the visitor around or give an introduction to the museum. Booklets can often be bought to explain the exhibits. These alternative formats are often used to provide information about the exhibits, replacing traditional museum labels which can be off-putting for many audiences.

As with archives and libraries, museum stewardship has become increasingly professional. Qualifications in curatorship are required and there are professional standards that most museums aim to achieve. Museums, as with archives, will have a collection policy, stating what they do accept and what they do not – a far cry from the rather haphazard collecting of the past. The policy may be determined by geography or by type of item. Items may be bought, donated or loaned from its owner. Professional conservators work to repair damaged items (often employed on a part-time basis or shared with other institutions).

Contents on display are not static. Museums often have special displays on particular topics, perhaps to commemorate an anniversary or highlight a certain feature of its collections. These displays will be temporary; perhaps lasting a few weeks or months, and may feature items from collections held elsewhere or from the public.

Museums should not be viewed merely as an entertaining experience for a weekend. What must also be realised is that the majority of a museum's holdings are not on display but in storage. This is because there is insufficient room to display all their possessions. Yet there should be listings of the museum's complete holdings. Often some of these can be viewed by appointment.

Museums offer the researcher an additional dimension of our ancestors' lives that other sources cannot. They allow the viewing and, on occasion, the touching of artefacts. These may include agricultural and industrial tools and other material.

Of the national museums, the Museum of English Rural Life based at Reading University (a university which specialises in agricultural matters) should be mentioned, because it is the national museum for life and work in the countryside. It was founded in 1951 and its purpose

Dr Johnson's House Museum. (Paul Lang)

is to record every aspect of English farming in particular. There was concern that the changing nature of agriculture would result in the disappearance of farming implements from usage. Apart from such tools and equipment, costume, veterinary equipment and evidence of country crafts are also collected. Along with three-dimensional objects, there is also a vast collection of photographs, oral history and written eye-witness accounts of life in the countryside. It also holds collections relating to wages of farm workers over time. In all these endeavours, help of country people is essential to provide information as well as exhibits.

The National Railway Museum at York is an essential place to visit, not only for railway enthusiasts but for anyone who has railwaymen among their ancestors. There is a large photographic archive there as well as technical records of trains and rolling stock. For those whose London ancestors worked for the railways or buses (or rode on them), the London Transport Museum is worth a visit. There are a number of trams, buses and underground trains which one can enter (at least in part). Another industry which created a great deal of employment for our ancestors was the canals. The Gloucester Waterways Museum and the Canal Museum in London have relevant collections, including examples of narrow boats and other paraphernalia associated with these craft and the people who worked on them.

Folk museums have existed in Britain since the 1930s. They aim to collect, preserve and make available items of little financial value, but which serve to illustrate a period of history of a particular part of the country. These items were once common, everyday objects which existed in large quantities. However, given technological advances, these are no longer used and so are in danger of being made extinct. Their display is enhanced if they are placed in a house of the period of which they are representative. These museums were first established on the continent and Britain was a late starter in this field.

One of England's first was the York Castle Museum, which opened just before the Second World War, in the buildings of the now disused county gaol. It reproduces an early Victorian cobbled street in York with shop frontages and interiors, showing everyday artefacts and products. There are also craftsmen's workshops with appropriate tools. The actual buildings therein are purpose-built, though the items on display are not.

Two other Yorkshire folk museums are the West Yorkshire Folk Museum at Shibden Hall, Halifax, and Kirkstall Abbey Museum near Leeds. Shibden Hall boasts agricultural and dairying equipment housed in a Pennine Barn, a collection of coaches and other vehicles and a number of craftsmen's workshops. Kirkstall, in the 1950s, recreated a

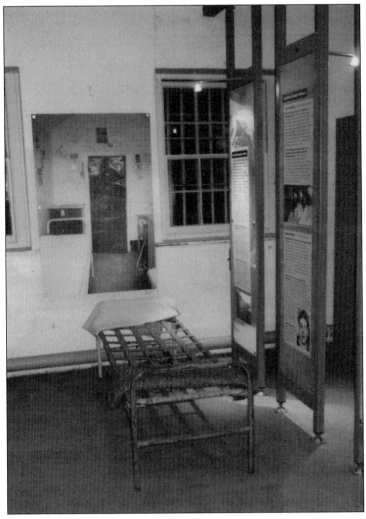

Interior of Oxford Prison Museum. (Author)

bygone urban environment, akin to the York Castle Museum, including a number of shops and workshops. These are a stationer's, an apothecary's, a haberdasher's, a blacksmith's, a wheelwright's and many others. There is also a collection of agrarian tools, oral history recordings and photographs of old crafts and their practitioners.

126

Some museums are formed out of now redundant buildings and aim to tell the history of the building. One example is Oxford Castle Prison, which was the county gaol from the early modern period until 1996. Many of the cells with original furniture and fittings are still in situ, along with explanation boards about prison routine, famous prisoners and trials and reminiscences of former prisoners. For those whose ancestors were employed in the prison or were incarcerated there, this can help illuminate part of their lives (parts of prisons still in use can sometimes be accessed for a visit by appointment; at Wandsworth Prison the now defunct condemned cell is usually a highlight – it is a claustrophobic experience).

Museums also hold two-dimensional items, too, for many predate record offices (which, apart from the National Archives, are largely a twentieth-century phenomenon). They collected paintings, photographs, ephemera and even archival material at time when no other institution did so. These may well be unique and it is always worth making an enquiry.

Horsham Museum, 2014. (Author)

Museums sometimes have special events such as talks by experts, displays by re-enactors and children's events, sometimes to mark specific anniversaries. These are opportunities to learn more and to talk to people who are experts in their subjects.

CASE STUDY
Horsham Museum

This is located in a sixteenth-century house in the town centre (Causeway House), once the home of the diarist Sarah Hurst, and has existed there since 1941, though it had moved from earlier sites, being founded in 1893. It has been run by the district council since 1974. It has three floors made up of 18 galleries. As with many museums, it had initially taken almost anything which was offered, which accounts for the ethnography collection, but in more recent times has had a more focused collection policy. The galleries include a room of children's toys and games, one of shoes, another of costumes and one of 'foreign objects'.

There are also rooms which focus on local history. These include rooms showing examples of local shops, local trade and industry (including saddles and ceramics), crime and punishment (including the door of a former police cell and a comb once owned by John George Haigh), and an illustrated history of the town. There are also non-permanent exhibitions; in December 2014 these included one of Paddington Bear and another of photographs of the district in the 1920s.

As well as these items, there is also a library of local books, 1,400 posters, 6,000 photographs, 500 paintings and prints and over 26,000 documents dating from the twelfth century onwards. It has a special collection of papers of nearby Warham-born poet Percy Shelley and prints by local artist John Millais, including some of fighting game cocks. The museum has a shop selling books and souvenirs of local interest and has knowledgeable and helpful staff.

There is educational provision for schools, including tours by the education officer. For the elderly in residential homes there are reminiscence boxes which can be lent out to them. The museum's website www.horsham.museum.org provides a virtual tour of the museum gallery by gallery.

While local history museums may have no documentation relating to your specific family, they will have material which can explain or evoke the life of your ancestors. The sort of help which a museum might give to the family historian includes dating family photographs from the clothing worn, or the style of writing on the back; photographs or paintings showing how your house, street or town looked in the past; plans or brochures for your house or housing estate; photos or other material relating to local schools; recorded memories of people who lived in your area or worked in the same occupation as one of your ancestors, information or artefacts connected with one of your ancestors if they were well-known locally; clothing of the type and date of those worn by your ancestors; tools, brochures or products from a business where your ancestor worked.

Since most museums have only a small staff and have most of their collections in storage, it is advisable to email or ring the museum first to ask if they have anything relevant to your enquiries and if these items are on show. If they are not, it will be necessary to make an appointment to see them.

Chapter 11

THE ORIGINS AND DEVELOPMENT OF LOCAL HISTORY

Finally, it may be worth taking a look at how local history has developed in England over the last few centuries. British history was a subject of interest to both Roman historians and, later, to Saxon and medieval monastic chroniclers. Their topics, though, were often national, mythological or religious, with Geoffrey of Monmouth writing the fictional *History of the Kings of Britain* in the twelfth century. It was only in the late fifteenth and sixteenth centuries that authors began to collect material for what would later be termed local history (at about the same time as there began, among the newly rich, an interest in genealogy, with heralds' visitations resulting in the construction of not always accurate pedigrees – the birth of family history). It was a time of great national upheaval as the Tudor age heralded the end of the Middle Ages and the end of the dominance of the Catholic Church in Britain. Perhaps one of the chief differences between local and family historians is that the latter do not usually publish their findings because they are deemed to be only of interest to the researcher and their immediate family, whereas local historians aim to have their work brought to the attention of a wider audience through being published in some form, for a history of a town or county is likely to have an appeal to all residents past and present.

The first people to study local history in England were those who made journeys through some or all of the country, titled itineraries. William of Worcester has been identified as the first. He made tours and recorded what he saw on them, especially about significant buildings but also the streets and lanes of his native Bristol, between 1477 and 1480. Another was John Leland in the first half of the next century, during the period of radical change when the monasteries were dissolved. His writings were not published until two centuries later, but they were far more substantial than Worcester's and are still of value today.

It was only at the end of the sixteenth century that people began to write what we would recognise as local history. They wrote not about the whole of the country or several parts of it, but concentrated on just one district. William Lambarde wrote the first history of an English county, *The Perambulation of Kent* in 1570. Two decades later, John Norden had his histories of Middlesex and Hertfordshire published. Throughout the seventeenth and eighteenth centuries others followed suit and so by 1800 there were few English counties which lacked a published history. Some had more than one and some were multi-volume. The Revd Daniel Lysons wrote several volumes of a history of the counties around London at the end of the eighteenth century, divided into chapters, each based on an individual parish.

These historians consulted various sources in order to have the evidence to write what they did, rather than rely solely on the evidence of their eyes as William of Worcester and John Leland had. Some used parish records, for example. Others relied on archives made available to them by senior clergy and officials. Personal observation still counted, however. These books were often very narrow in their scope. The authors were usually gentry, and, increasingly, clergymen, who had the time, leisure, contacts and education in order to research and write. They tended to concentrate on noble and gentle families and their lineage, and on the landed estates of the county in question. Churches and clergymen also figure prominently, as does manorial history. Economic and social history, and that of the bulk of the population, was often neglected, unless there is something exceptionally unusual, such as a man living to 114 or a clergyman baptising a female child Thomas.

This tradition continued until at least the nineteenth century, even among authors who were not from the social elite. One such was Thomas Faulkner (1777–1855), who ran a bookseller's and stationery shop in London, but also wrote several books about different parishes in Middlesex and West London from 1810 to 1839. He concentrated on the nobility, gentry and clergy, recording their inscriptions in parish churches and focusing on their lives – of course the descendants of these people were his main customers.

The development of county histories led to that of town histories. John Stow's *Survey of London*, of 1598, was the first. He acknowledged his inspiration lay with the county historians. Yet books concerning towns and cities were less numerous than those of counties. Ralph Thoresby's history of Leeds in 1715 was the first of any Yorkshire town or city; others soon followed in his wake.

Thomas Faulkner, local historian. (London Borough of Ealing)

Choosing a smaller scope, but at a deeper level, was the parish. The Revd White Kennett was the first parish historian in 1695, with his *History of Ambrosden and other adjacent parts*. Other clergymen followed his lead. Not all parish historians were clergy; John Lucas, a Leeds schoolmaster from Lancashire, wrote a history of Warton, his parish of birth, in the early eighteenth century, though this was not published for another two centuries (a not uncommon occurrence for some early local historians).

A good example of the content of these early histories and their source material can be found in the introduction to the first volume of the Revd Daniel Lyson's *Environs of London*, first published in 1790, and described by the author as 'Advertisement':

> Whilst a taste for local history so generally prevails, it is somewhat singular that the counties adjacent to London should not have had their due share of illustration; for even in those of which histories have been published, some very interesting particulars have been wholly unnoticed. The author of the following work offers to the public what he has been able to collect, relating either to the ancient history or present state of the several parishes within twelve miles of the capital, a district which furnishes perhaps more curious and interesting matter for observation than any other of the same extent of the kingdom. A brief description of the situation, soil, produce, and manufactures; the descent of the principal, particularly manerial [sic] property; the parish churches, and ecclesiastical history; the state of

population, and the biography connected with each parish; are the principal objects of the following work.

Through the obliging permission of Thomas Astle, Esq. John Caley, Esq. and John Kipling, Esq. to inspect the Records of the Tower, the Augmentation Office, and the Rolls; through the politeness of the present proprietors of the several manors, and the ready and liberal assistance of the gentlemen of the law; the author has been enabled to give the descent of property in a manner which, though brief, he hopes will be found accurate. In the description of parish churches, those epitaphs only are given at length, which are either singular in themselves, or record persons of eminence, and these have been all copied on the spot; from the others he has inserted the names of the persons recorded, with the dates of their decease, merely to denote the place of their interment of the several families. In treating of the ecclesiastical history, an account is given of the nature of the benefice of each parish, and, where it could be ascertained, the descent of the advowson. In this department, the frequent references to the MSS. in the Lambeth library will shew how much the author has been indebted to his Grace the Archbishop of Canterbury, for his permission to consult them. The succession of incumbents on each benefice has not been given, on a presumption, that a bare list of names would be very uninteresting to the reader, and tend to swell the volume to very little purpose; the author has confined himself therefore to the noticing of such persons only as have been in any respect eminent. The parochial registers (for a ready access to which, as well as for other occasional information, he is much indebted to his brethren the clergy) have been found of much assistance in ascertaining the comparative state of population and furnishing hints for biographical matter. The ravages of the plague in many of the parishes at various periods, have been ascertained from the same source of information; and such instances of longevity as are there recorded, have been also noticed. From the churchwardens accounts, particularly at Lambeth and Kingston, several curious circumstances, relating to the price of provisions, and local customs, have been extracted.

The difficulty of correctness in a work of this nature, wherein the references are necessarily so numerous, is well known. The reader, it is hoped, will excuse such trifling inaccuracies as may have escaped the author's observation; especially as he has endeavoured to correct those which are material, particularly in the references to public records, which have been …

Apart from a narrow focus, other early local historians were happy to repeat myths and legends as if they were true, if they were sufficiently interesting. Thus John Allan Brown of Ealing wrote *Greenford Parva* in 1894 and included a lengthy chapter on the Ghost of Perivale Mill, which lacks contemporary source material. William King Baker in 1912 in his *History of Acton* included pages about figures from national history (Oliver Cromwell, Richard Baxter and the third Earl of Derwentwater) whose connection with his subject was fleeting at best. Of the industries which had been established in the town in recent decades he said virtually nothing.

Local historians were from a narrow stratum of society. They were almost all male, often with a university background at a time when very few participated in higher education. Many were gentry or clergy, or had the wealth to have the time for study and writing. They also needed the right contacts as well as the right education, as access to documents was limited. They had to have the wealth and/or contacts to have their work published. Many had an interest in genealogy, interestingly enough. Ralph Thoresby claimed his family could be traced back to the early eleventh century and it was not uncommon to reproduce the descents of major county families within their books, as appears in Edmund Hasted's *History of the County of Kent*.

All this is now known as the antiquarian tradition. Despite its limitations, it should not be despised nor ignored. First, the authors often reproduce documents or describe places or inscriptions which now do not exist and therefore they have collected unique material within their books. Secondly, their comments about their own times are valuable in themselves as providing evidence of contemporary attitudes.

Publication of local history books needed money and many authors were not able to provide for such out of their own means. They therefore solicited subscriptions from the social elite of the county or town/city in which they were writing, and the names of nobility, gentry and clergy are often inscribed at the beginning of the book, as they paid for their copies in advance and so covered the costs of publication. Therefore it made sense for the author to devote much of the book to the descent and activities of the social elite of the district.

Academic rigour was increasingly brought to bear on the writing of local history at the end of the nineteenth century. This was in the form of the *Victoria History of the Counties of England* (known as the *VCH*), with its ambitious aim to produce a properly sourced history of each parish in each county in England. It was initially and optimistically envisaged that this would be a 160-volume series and would be completed within six years. As with much local history publication, it was initially financed by subscriptions (headed by Queen Victoria). By 1908, 50 volumes had been produced. It was taken over by the Institute of Historical Research, part of the University of London, in 1933 and is now partly financed by the local authorities whose territories under survey are part of its jurisdiction. The plan was to have two or three introductory volumes covering chapters devoted to themes drawing from the county's history; prehistoric, geological, agricultural, political, educational, sporting and so on. Then there would be a parish by parish survey, with each volume covering a number of parish histories. Many of the early volumes (e.g. Buckinghamshire, Lancashire, Hampshire, Hertfordshire and Bedfordshire) were not dissimilar to what had been written in the past: a focus on the (highly detailed) descent of landed families, of manors and estates, of the parish church and the clergy, followed by a list of parish charities, often established by the aforesaid squires and parsons. The actual history of the parish and its people was often neglected in these accounts. Yet they are often well illustrated with photographs and contain copies of early street plans and plans of churches, cathedrals, castles and large houses. They also note the source of information given in the text. Work on these volumes was in the hands of local county committees and local historians.

In more recent volumes, chiefly those post-1945, the contents of the series are far different and cover various themes such as communications, economic and social history, religious, charitable and educational history. They are written by professional historians. The information included is sourced to enable the interested reader to follow them up. The series is still being published, and there is now no clear idea when completion will occur. These histories are not meant as the last word on the subject, but rather as a useful framework for further research. Most of the volumes can now be read and searched online.

Some counties, such as Northumberland (a county history committee for this county produced its own volumes of county history, very much in the antiquarian tradition) and Westmorland, have not been covered at all, and some, such as Cumberland and Kent only have the introductory volumes covering the survey of the county. However, Essex, Middlesex, Lancashire and Cheshire have had many volumes devoted to their history. This series represents the best introduction to the history of a particular county or parish.

One issue was that the writing of history in past centuries was the work of antiquarians as opposed to historians proper. An antiquarian was a collector of facts, often very valuable in themselves, but which were laid out in text without any discernment as to what was of value and what was not, and without much analysis or narrative – in short, not history, but the materials for history. This sort of 'history' is by no means confined to the past and antiquarianism still lives on.

There was further interest in local history in the 1920s and 1930s. A small number of universities ran extension lectures in local history, chiefly on individual buildings. The new University College of Hull, in 1929, had a Chair of Adult Education. Tutors were employed to give lectures in villages about the local history of the locality; in two instances these resulted in short courses of a dozen lectures. Summer courses were established, often including visits to buildings of interest. Many of those attending became part-time tutors. War interrupted such activities but did not kill them off.

Since the Second World War there has been an upsurge in interest in local history. Local history societies were formed, often for villages and towns, as well as the more established county history societies. In 1948 the first standing conference for local history was established to encourage the study of local history and bring together representatives of local history committees (which rose from 13 in 1948 to 43 in 1973). Universities began to offer degree courses in local history (one of the pioneers being Leicester University in 1949 under the aegis of Professor W G Hoskins) and adult evening courses in the subject were being offered by colleges, the Workers' Education Association, and less formally, under the aegis of village groups such as parish councils and Women's Institutes.

Regional history has also been a topic of interest. For example, Lancashire University had a Centre for North Western Regional Studies.

This published works which covered historical topics with an impact of the whole 'region' (such as this author's *Responses to the Jacobite Invasion of 1745 in North West England*). Journals such as *Southern History*, *Northern History* and *Midlands History* were established (in 1979, 1965 and 1971 respectively) to publish articles and review books which covered aspects of the history of these regions, cutting across county and parish boundaries. Generally these were the province of 'professional' historians rather than those whose interest in local history is that of a hobbyist.

An important publication, *The Amateur Historian*, renamed *The Local Historian* in 1968, was published from 1952, which included articles about various topics related to local history as well as reviews of the increasing number of books on the subject. The editorial of the first issue stated:

> During the last few years, there has been a great increase in the interest shown in history. In Britain, perhaps more than in any other country, we have always tended to look upon our history as part of our personality; but during the war the threat to our way of life and our ancient cities turned particular attention to the past from which our traditions have stemmed. With the removal of that threat, the interest has not lessened; rather with the records once more available, it has flowered into a widespread active curiosity about our history, and particularly the history of our towns and villages.

Articles included therein tend to be of two types. First, there are those which cover a particular source for local history, such as maps, photographs and oral history, or discuss sources relevant to a particular topic. Then there are articles about particular people, places or events which concern aspects of local history. Finally there are book reviews about books relevant to the study of local history or of local history books. Anyone seriously interested in local history should read these (they are now published quarterly); most record offices and some libraries subscribe to the journal.

Local historians had been chiefly gentlemen and clergy in previous centuries but in more recent decades have become rather more diverse. They include professionals: archivists, librarians, museum curators, archaeologists, teachers and academics. But they also include those for whom history is not their profession, but a hobby. They tend to come from professional backgrounds, often with a degree, sometimes retired, but with a great enthusiasm for the subject.

Local history books were written in larger numbers than ever before. Some publishers commissioned whole series of books, of varying kinds. One popular choice is the publication of books of old photographs of a particular town, often based on old postcard collections, with captions of varying lengths. There were also more textual books, though usually highly illustrated, as well. These were often written by librarians, archivists and others with historical training. There is, however, no comprehensive coverage. Many villages are without adequate histories or only have very elderly ones which have inevitably missed more recent decades, which have often been periods of change as great as any in the past. Even generally good books have virtually nothing to say of recent decades. (John Coulter's *Lewisham: History and Guide*, published in 1994, says nothing about the town's last three decades and very little about the twentieth century; 'a catalogue of disasters' notes the author. Frances Hounsell's *Greenford, Northolt and Perivale Past*, published five years later, treats its history as ending in about 1950.) Whether this is a defect or not is a matter of opinion, but once the period in question ceases to remain in living memory it certainly will be.

Bookshops, libraries and museums should sell the more recently published of these books. They may also be found on online book sites, though for out of print ones abebooks is recommended, as well as the dwindling number of second-hand bookshops.

Local history societies have flourished since the early nineteenth century. One of their functions has always been to enable like minded people to meet and to share their findings in convivial surroundings. Originally often restricted by class and sex, they are now open to anyone who has an interest in the subject. These societies have regular meetings where either an outside speaker gives a talk or one of its members does, on a topic which is relevant to the district's local history. It is worth ascertaining if there is such a society which covers the district that your ancestors came from (local libraries or record offices should know of any) and what their talk schedule is. Even if the topic is not of obvious interest, for example, a talk about the brass industry in Birmingham, but your ancestors there were jewellers, then it may still be worth venturing along because it will give you a chance to meet with members whose research interests may coincide with yours and so you may gain invaluable research tips which might have taken longer to discover. Not all towns and counties have a local history society, but many do; they may be titled archaeological or antiquarian societies, but usually their remit is wider than the title suggests. Societies vary considerably: some are recent creations and some date back over a century, some produce an impressive range of publications, others do not. Some have informative websites, but not all.

Local history societies have risen and some have collapsed over the years, due to lack of local support or as members die off. Even where there is not a local history society in existence, there is usually a local historian or two. Their knowledge and accessibility is certainly diverse, but their enthusiasm is usually immense because this is one of their passions in life.

It is important that anyone investigating local and family history should have an informed knowledge on national history. National developments, such as legislation, wars and rebellions, have an impact on communities and so an awareness of these is important. Otherwise it will lead to confusion and a lack of understanding. I recall a history of Deptford's Catholic church stating with amazement that the Catholics there were being maligned in a document published in 1745. When it is known that this was a year in which there was a dangerous rebellion which aimed to put a Catholic King on the throne, then all is made clear. Single-volume histories of England/Britain are easily available, as are specific volumes of different periods of history, which should give more detail.

Local history has a pedigree of several centuries. It has produced much, especially in recent decades, though this output has been variable in nature. Its products are of use, but should always be checked wherever that is possible (sometimes it is not, for original documents consulted in an earlier century may well have been subsequently lost or ceased to exist). It is now a topic that is researched and written about by both amateurs and professionals, aimed at diverse markets.

Yet it is not a separate world from family history. Several recent books aim to link the two, by stressing the link between family and community history. Names, dates and places make up a family tree, it has been argued, but family history is an extra and enlightening dimension, and that requires the family historian to study local history, too.

CONCLUSION

The sources for the study of local history, just like those for family history, are overlapping. Local history and family history also intersect and a knowledge of one can inform the other. For example, local newspapers, particularly for the twentieth century, may contain photographs which are duplicated in a collection of photographs of that locality. In the late nineteenth and early twentieth centuries, newspapers carried detailed reports of council meetings, which would also be found in the minute books of those same councils. Local histories will, or certainly should, derive their information from these archives, newspapers, photograph collections and other sources. A degree of repetition is inevitable. The same could be said about family history sources; the 1881 census will tell us that someone appearing on it will be ten years older than that same person in 1871.

Local history is not about individuals and families, unless they were very influential (usually meaning very rich and powerful). It is, or should be, primarily about a community and how that community changes over time. Yet that same community is made up of families and individuals. They cannot be separated and each has an impact on the other. It is impossible to fully realise the history of one without the other. Family historians, therefore, should explore the context of the local society in which their ancestors lived.

However, the researcher should not try to build too much on some of their findings. It is tempting to place your ancestors in the middle of especially exciting or well-known events in history which happened near to them. For example, having a London ancestor who was resident in 1649 does not automatically mean that they were present at Charles I's execution on 30 January of that year. Or having a Preston ancestor in 1715 does not mean that they were dodging musket balls during the battle there in November (they may well have fled the arrival of the armies before the fighting began). They would have been aware of these important events, but their actions, unless documented, cannot be stated with any certainty.

It is also worthwhile looking at the well-known genealogical sources again – at the census returns and parish registers, for example, from which the entries for your ancestors have already long been extracted. In the case of the former, it is worth asking who were your ancestors' neighbours? Did they have the same profession or were employed in the same industry or in different ones? Did they have large families or small ones? Were they born in the same town or village? Or for parish registers: who were the witnesses at the marriage? Were there other baptisms or burials at the same time as your ancestors'?

Local history sources, therefore, can add an extra dimension to the knowledge of your ancestors' lives and deaths by providing a background to them. They did not live in a vacuum any more than we do. Social, political, economic, religious and military events do influence people's lives, and not just major national and international ones. A council's decision to install street lighting in a town might be just as important to people's lives as zeppelin raids in the First World War. And, of course, you may find an additional reference to your family or to those who had a direct influence on their lives (e.g. teachers at the school your ancestor attended or a militia officer they may have served under).

You are not required to become a local historian and research and write the history of all the places where your ancestors lived. The choice is yours as to how far and how deep you want to dig to illuminate the lives of your ancestors. Hopefully this book has pointed out the possibilities and the pitfalls of such local history research and will lead you to know more of your ancestors' lives and context; after all, to paraphrase Kipling, 'What do they know of family history those who only family history know?'

USEFUL ADDRESSES

Archon Archives
Online directory
www.apps.nationalarchives.gov.uk/archon

Bodleian Library
Broad Street, Oxford OX13BG
Tel. 01865 277162
www.bodleian.ox.ac.uk
Email: reader.services@bodleian.ox.ac.uk

Borthwick Institute
University of York, Heslington, York YO10 5DD
Tel. 01904 321166
www.borthwick.york.ac.uk
Email: borthwick.institute@york.ac.uk

British Library
96 Euston Road, London NW1 2BD
Tel. 01937 546060
www.bl.uk

Chetham Library
Manchester M3 1SB
Tel. 0161 834 7961
www.chethams.org.uk

English Heritage Archive
Kemble Drive, Swindon, Wiltshire SN2 2GZ
Tel. 01793 414600
www.english.heritage.org.uk

Guildhall Library
Aldermanbury, London EC2V 7HH
Tel. 020 7332 1868/70
www.cityoflondon.gov.uk
Email: guildhall.library@cityoflondon.gov.uk

John Rylands Library
150 Deansgate, Manchester M3 3EH
Tel. 0161 306 0555
www.library.manchester.ac.uk/rylands
Email: uml.special-collections@manchester.ac.uk

Lambeth Palace Library
London SE1 7JU
Tel. 020 7898 1200
www.lambethpalacelibrary.org

Modern Records Centre
University Library, University of Warwick, Coventry CV4 7AL
Tel. 024 7652 4219
www2.warwick.ac.uk
Email: archives@warwick.ac.uk

Museum of English Rural Life
Whiteknights, University of Reading, Reading RG6 6AG
Tel. 0118 378 8660
www.reading.ac.uk/merl
Email: merl@reading.ac.uk

The National Archives
Ruskin Avenue, Kew, Richmond, Surrey TW9 4DU
Tel. 020 8876 3444
www.nationalarchives@gov.uk

Parliamentary Archives
Houses of Parliament, London SW1A 0PW
Tel. 020 7219 3074
www.parliament.uk
Email: archives@parliament.uk

This is a very select list of national and regional archives and libraries. Contact details of specific archives and libraries can be found on Archon (there seems no point in duplicating here that list of over 1,000 repositories in the UK). Do bear in mind that these institutions will not be able to do your work for you, but to answer enquiries on their holdings prior to a visit by yourself. Do always try to contact anywhere prior to a visit and order material in advance if possible, to avoid disappointment.

SELECT BIBLIOGRAPHY

This is a very general list of publications which cover a range of general topics for local history, concerning sources and methodology. They should be treated as being background reading to supplement the information already provided in this book. A complete list of local history publications and record society publications, or a complete bibliography of local history books or a list of local newspapers would take up an entire book (at least). Keyword searching the British Library's online catalogue Explore will supply a list of titles which match that keyword. Contacting or visiting the relevant county or borough archives should result in those relevant to the village, town or city that you are interested in.

Local History societies can be found at www.local-history.co.uk/ Groups.

J Beckett, *Writing Local History* (2007)

G Beech and R Mitchell, *Maps for Local and Family History* (2004)

J Black, *The English Press, 1621–1961* (2001)

R Carline, *Pictures in the Past: The Story of the Picture Postcard* (1971)

P Carter and K Thompson, *Sources for Local Historians* (2005)

S Caunce, *Oral History and the Local Historian* (1994)

C R J Currie and C P Lewis (eds), *English County Histories: A Guide* (1994)

H P R Finberg and J Thirsk (eds), *Agrarian History of England and Wales*, 8 vols (2001)

R Finnegan and M Drake (eds), *From Family Tree to Family Historian* (1994)

R Finnegan and J Eustace (eds), *Sources and Methods for Family and Community Historians* (1994)

S Fowler, *Starting out in Local History* (2001)

J Gibson and B Langton, *Local Newspapers, 1750–1920*, 3rd edn (2000)

J Golby (ed.), *Communities and Families* (1994)

J B Harley and C W Phillips, *The Historian's Guide to Ordnance Survey Maps* (1984)

D Hey, *Family History and Local History in England* (1987)
D Hey, *Journeys in Family History* (2004)
D Hey, *How our Ancestors Lived: A History of Life a Hundred Years Ago* (2004)
D Hey (ed.), *The Oxford Companion to Family and Local History* (2010)
P Hindle, *Maps for Historians* (1988)
W G Hoskins, *Local History in England* (1957)
K Howarth, *Oral History: A Handbook* (1998)
M Murphy, *Newspapers and Local History* (1991)
Museums and Galleries in Great Britain and Ireland (annual publication)
G Oliver, *Using Old Photographs: A Guide for Family Historians* (1989)
M Palmer and P Neaverson, *Industrial Archaeology Principles and Practice* (1994)
N Pevsner and others, *The Buildings of England* (1955 to date)
R Pryce (ed.), *From Family History to Community History* (1994)
M Richards, *The Encyclopedia of Ephemera* (2000)
J Richardson, *The Local Historians' Encyclopedia* (2003)
C D Rogers and J H Smith, *Local Family History in England* (1992)
D Smith, *Maps and Plans for Local Historian and Collector* (1988)
W E Tate, *The Parish Chest* (1969)
H Wallis (ed.), *Historian's Guide to Early British Maps* (1994)
J West, *Village Records* (1980)
J West, *Town Records* (1983)
Victoria County Histories (1900 to date); also on www.british-history.ac.uk

Journals (general, not county/town specific)
Agricultural History Review (1953 to date)
The Amateur Historian, later *The Local Historian* (1952 to date)
Industrial Archaeology Review (1976 to date)
Local History Magazine (1984 to date)
Local Population Studies (1968 to date)
Midlands History (1971 to date)
Northern History (1965 to date)
Southern History (1979 to date)

INDEX